MY
NAME

....

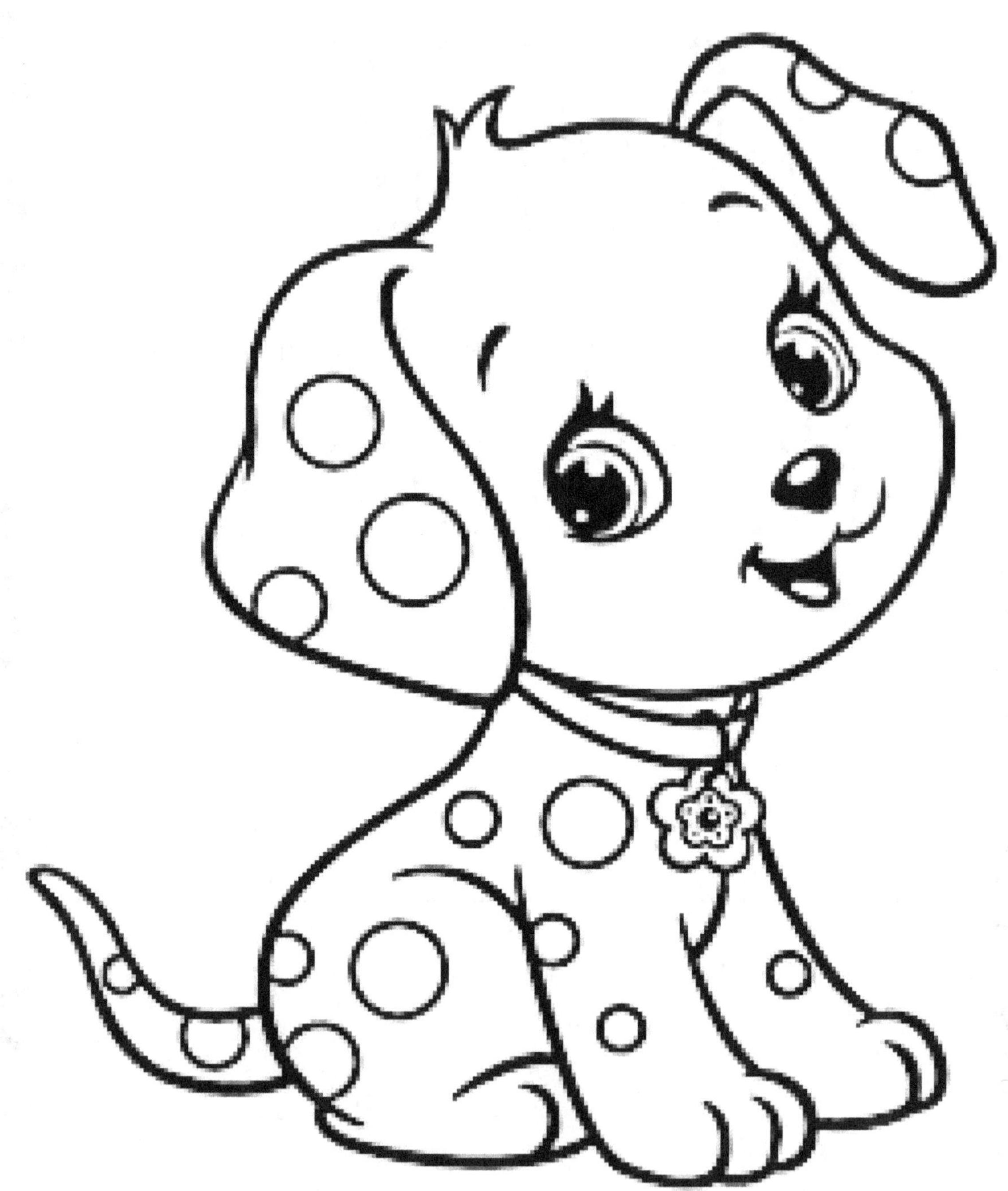

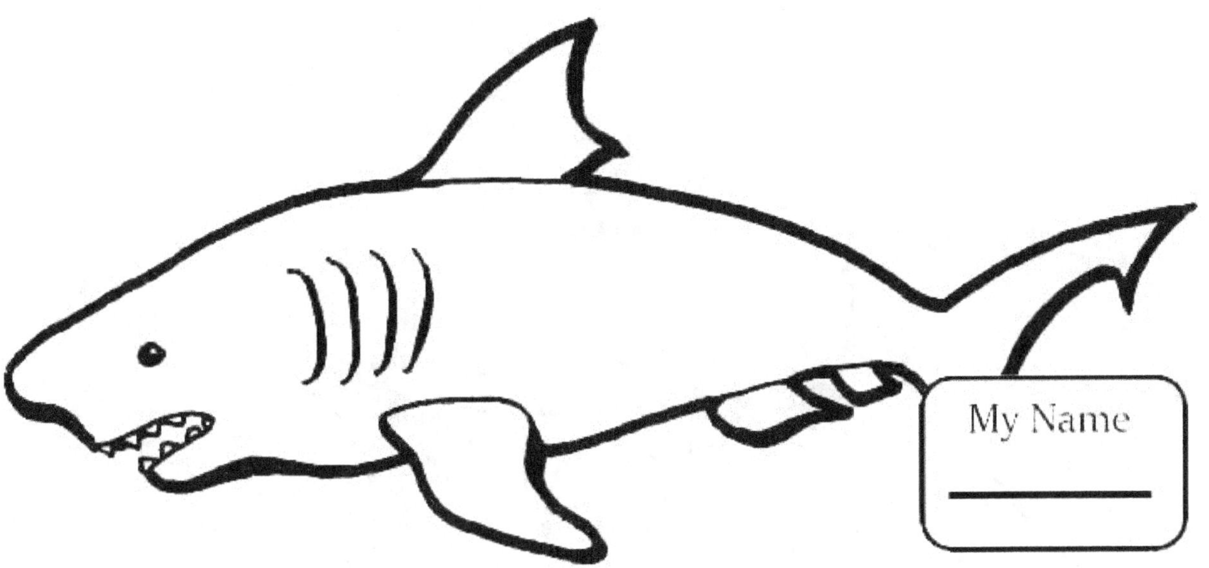

My Name

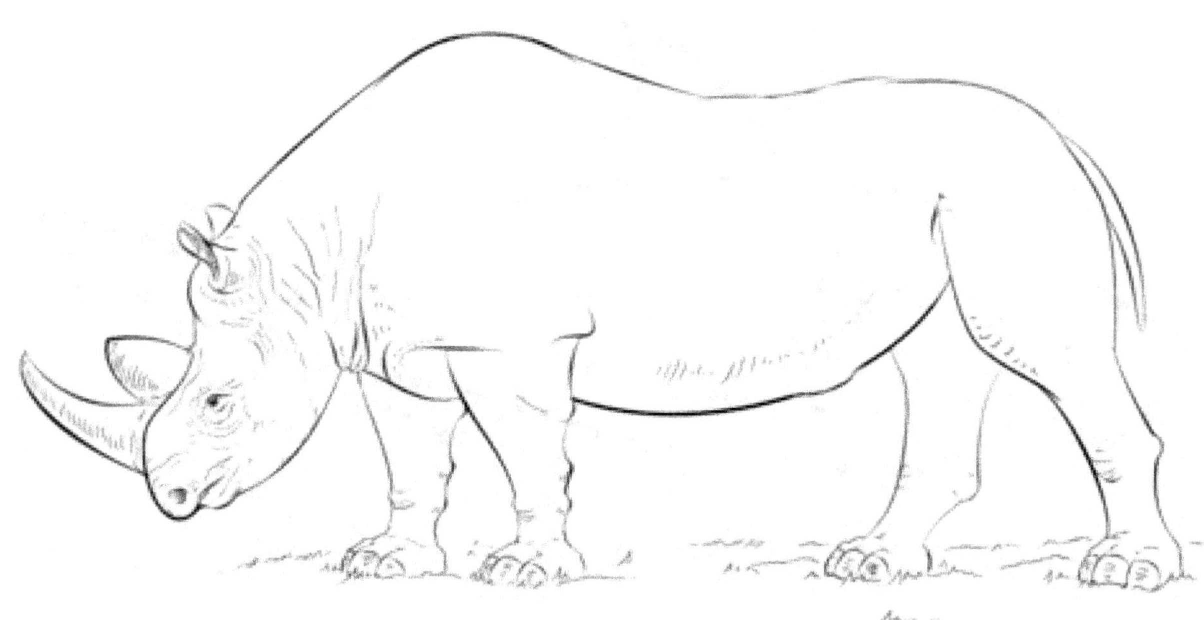

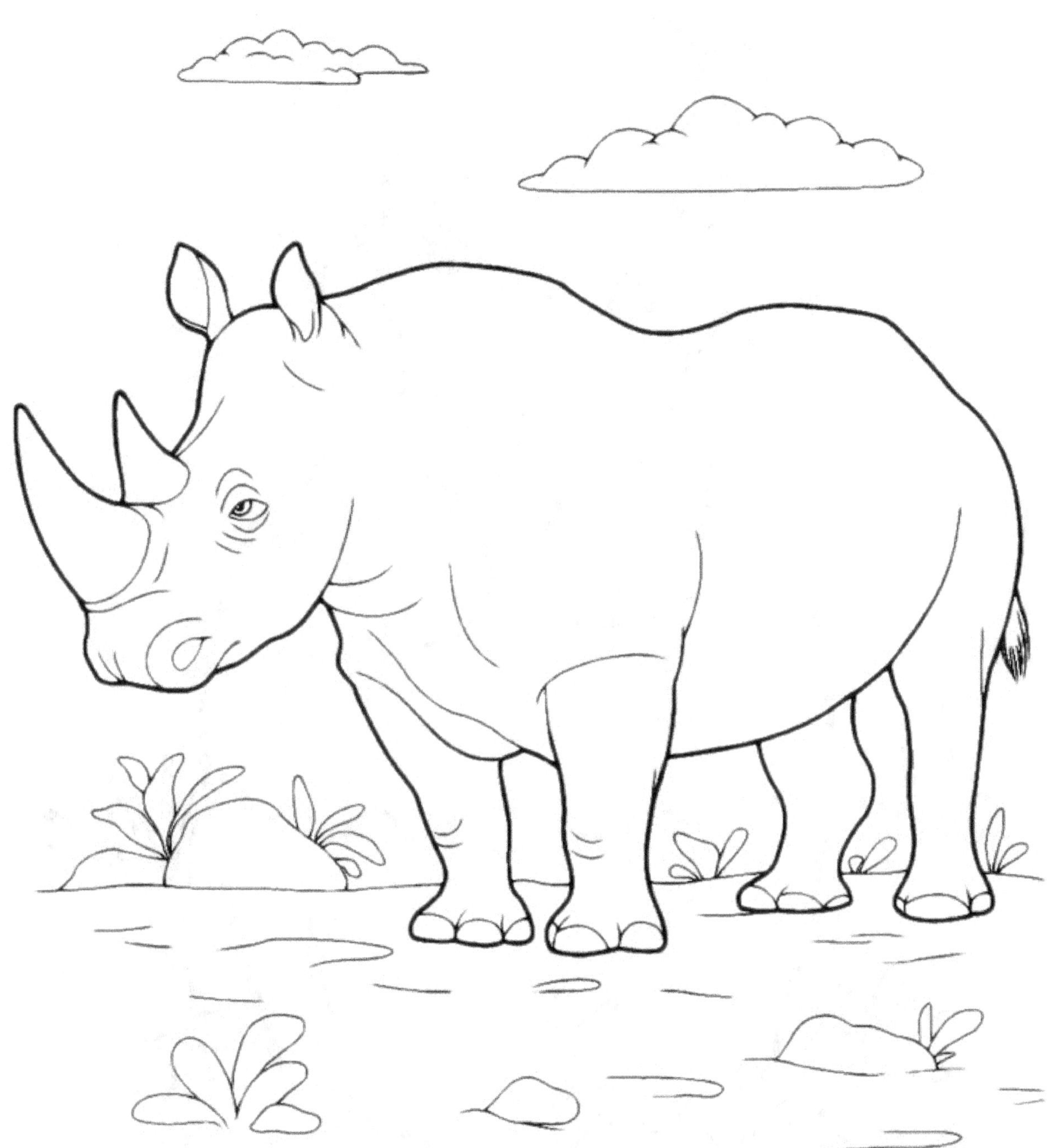

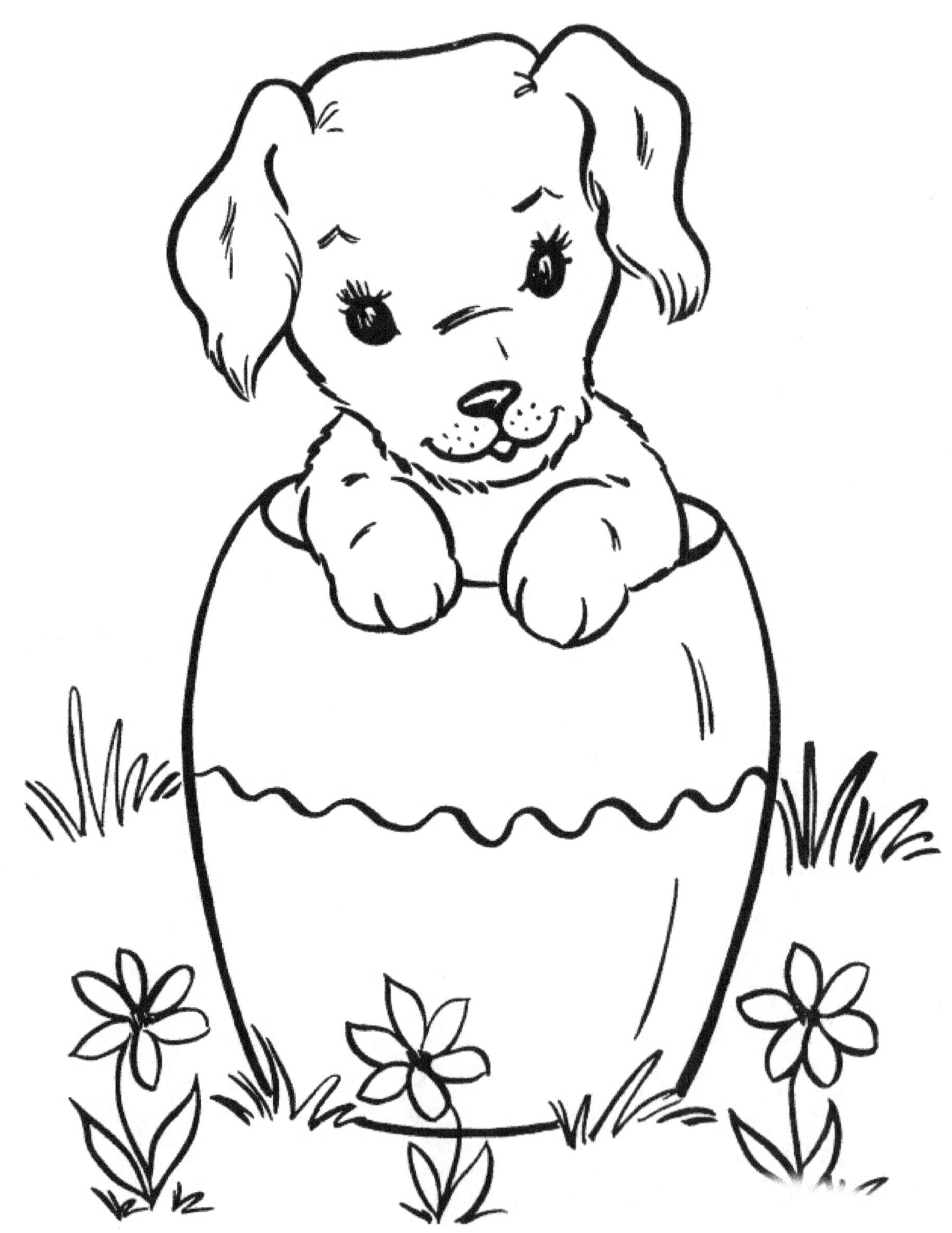

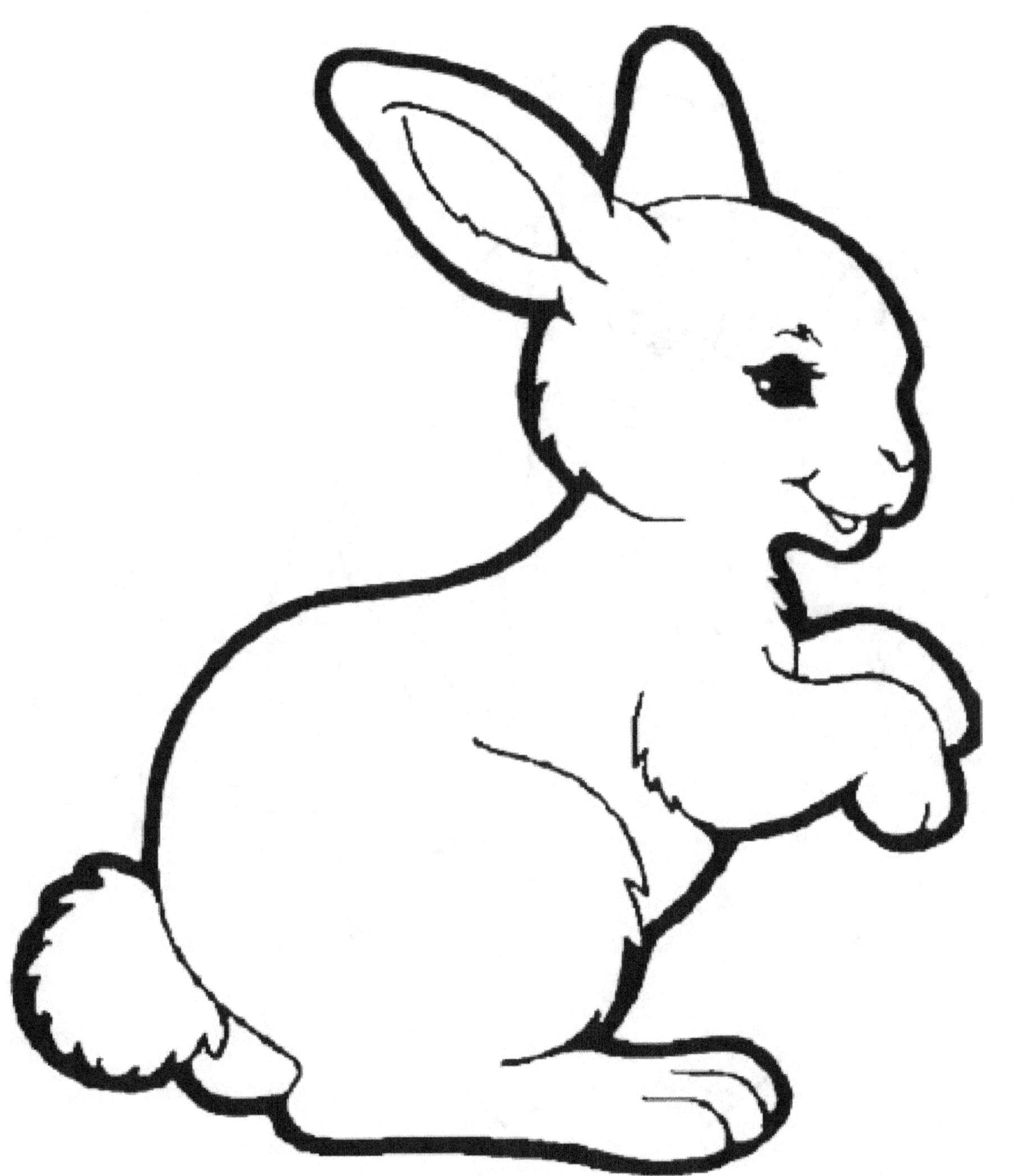

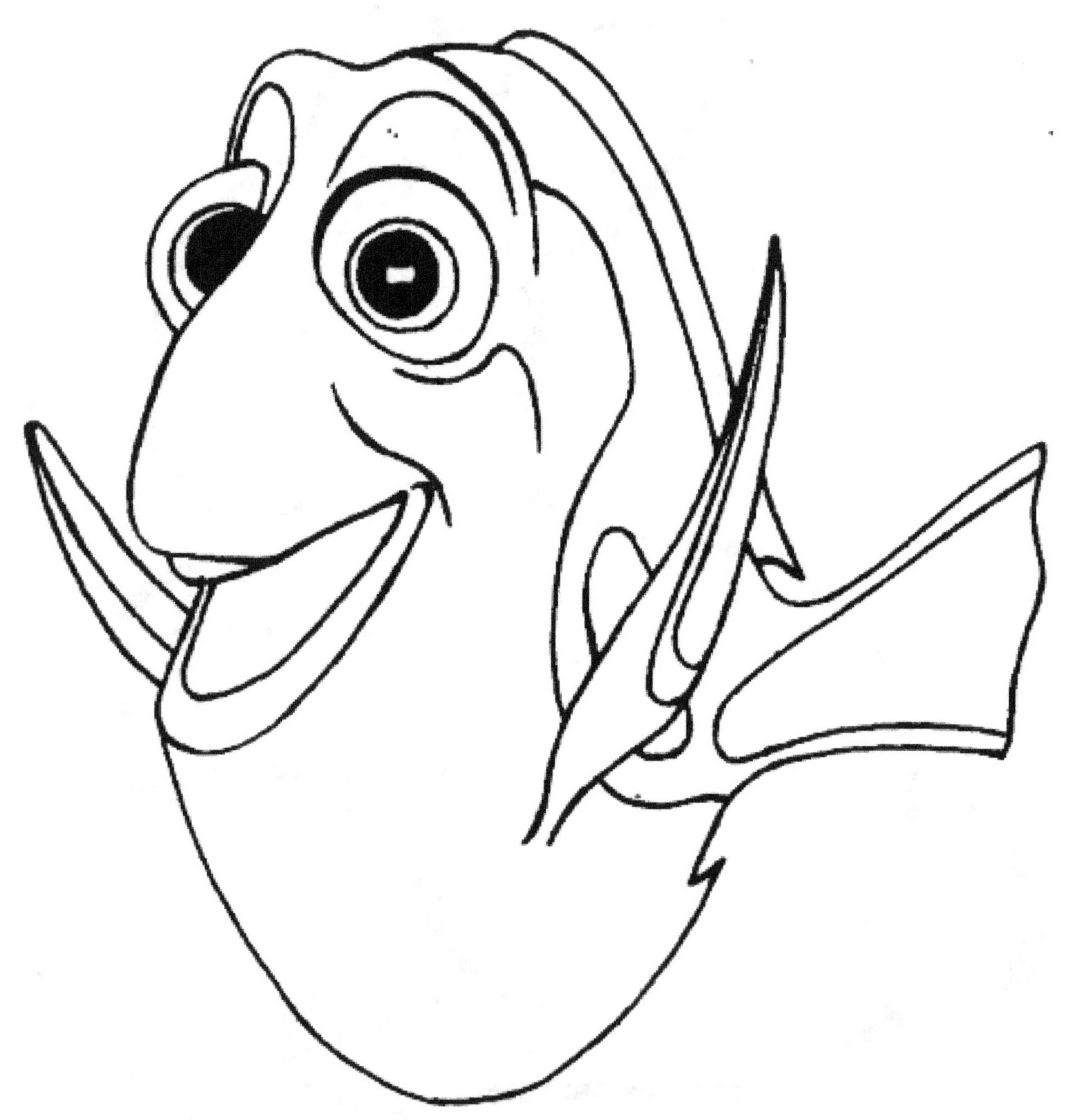

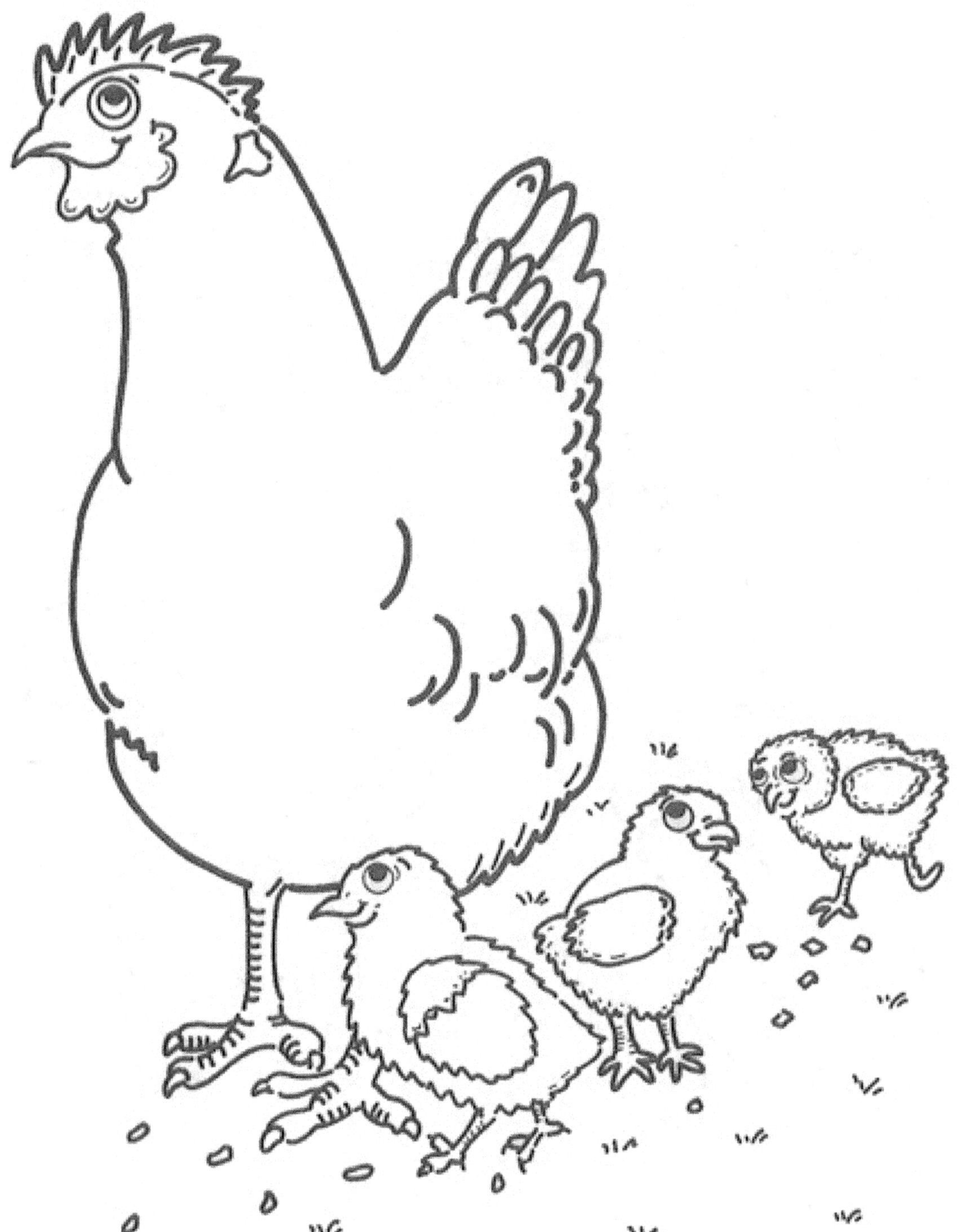

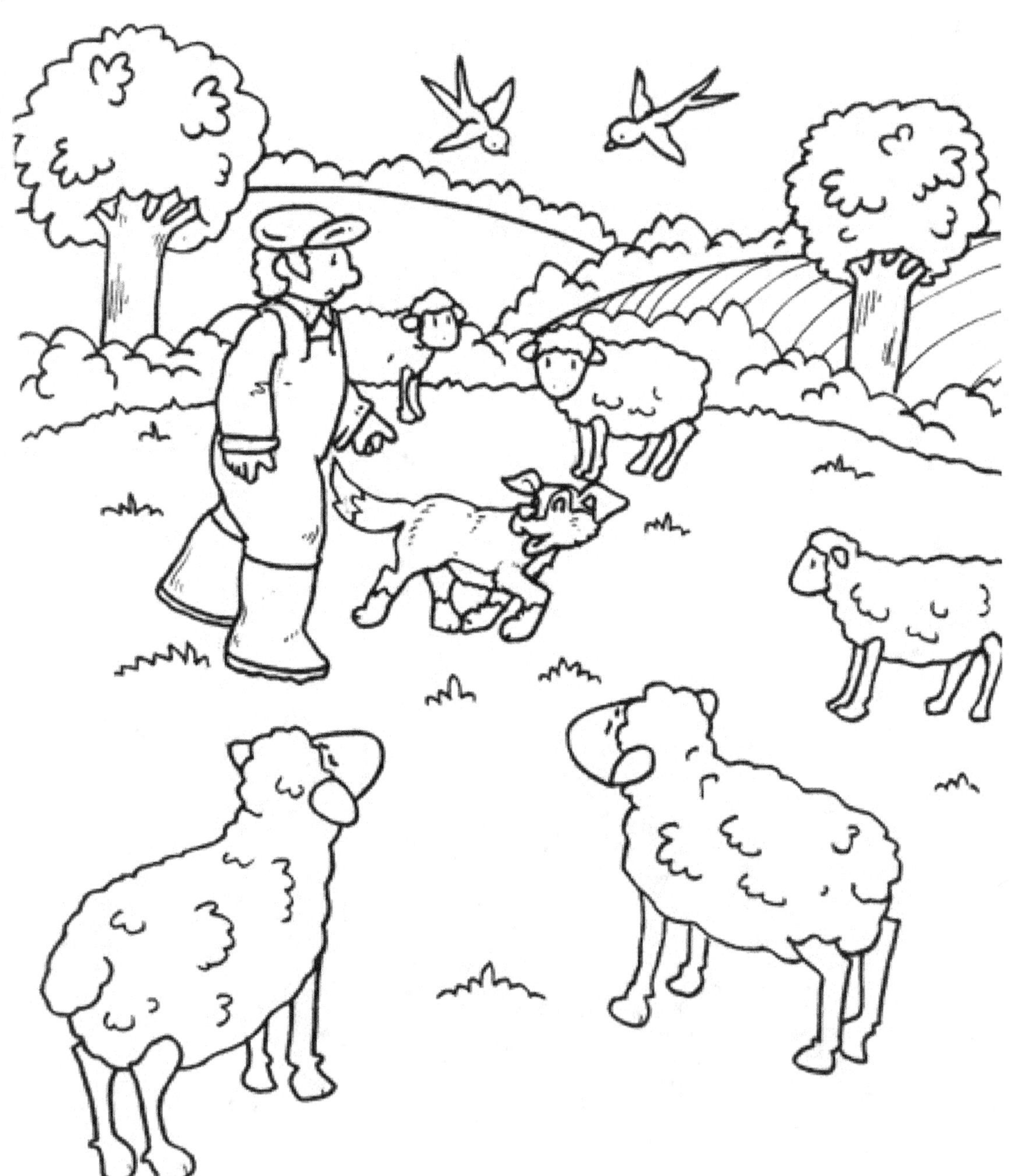

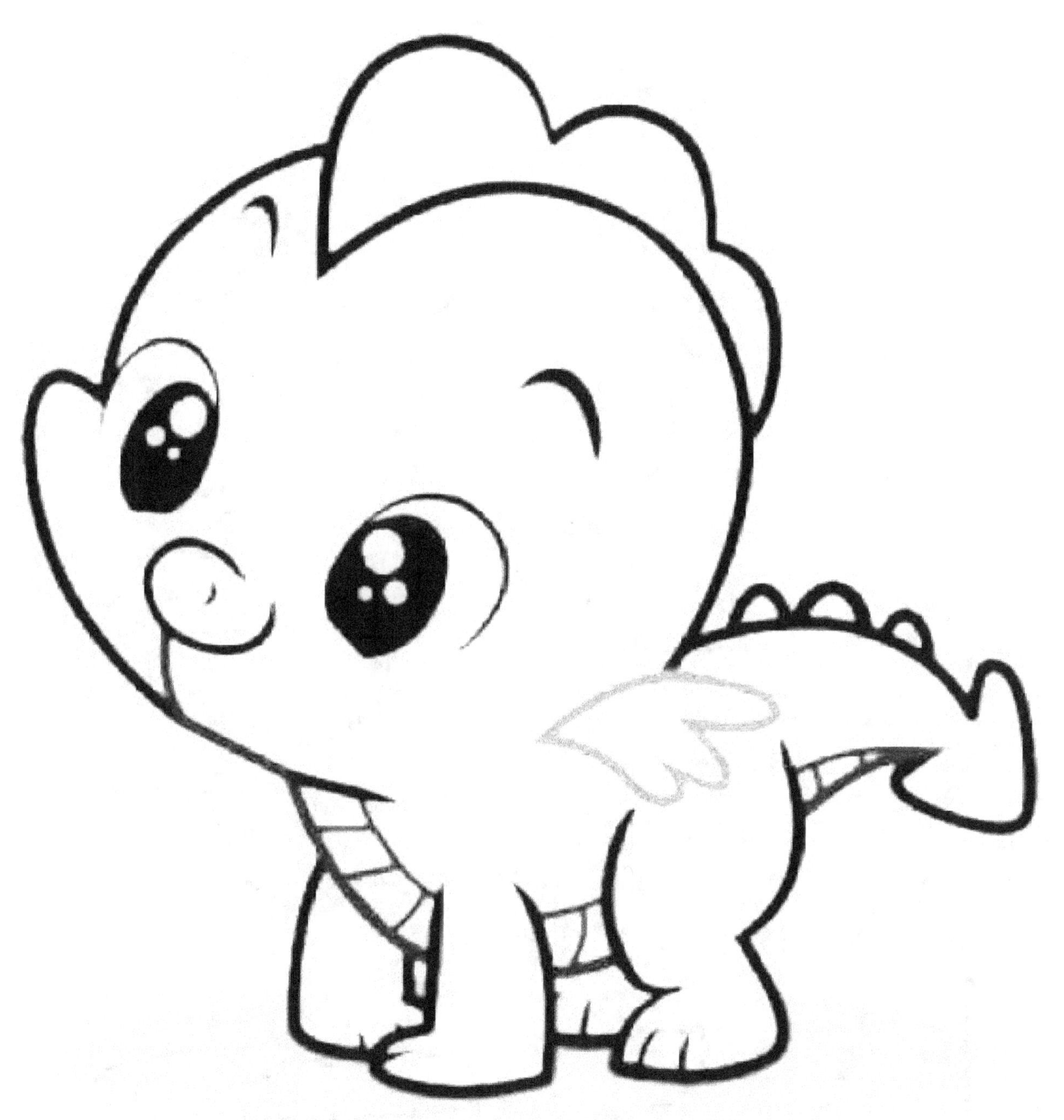

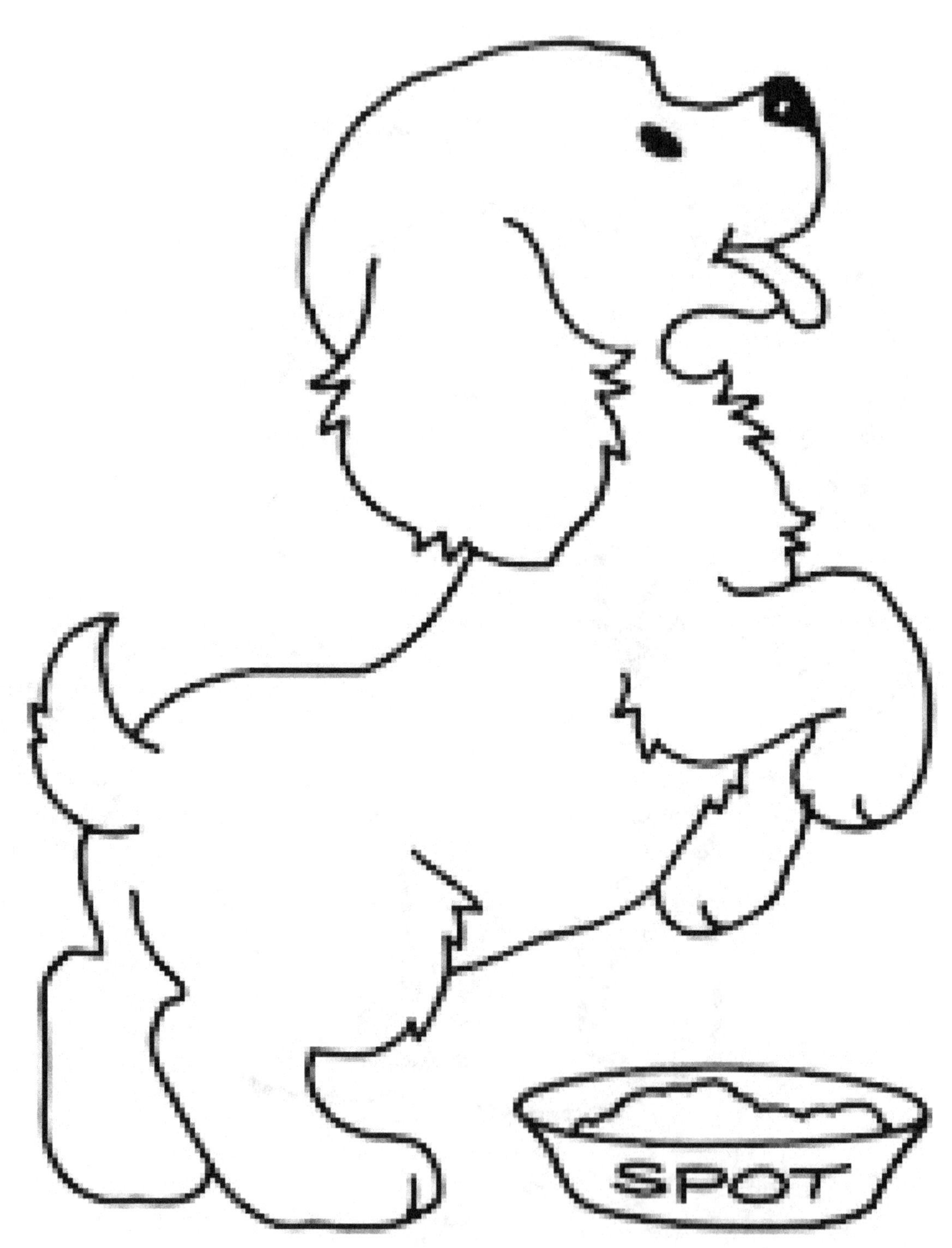

SPOT

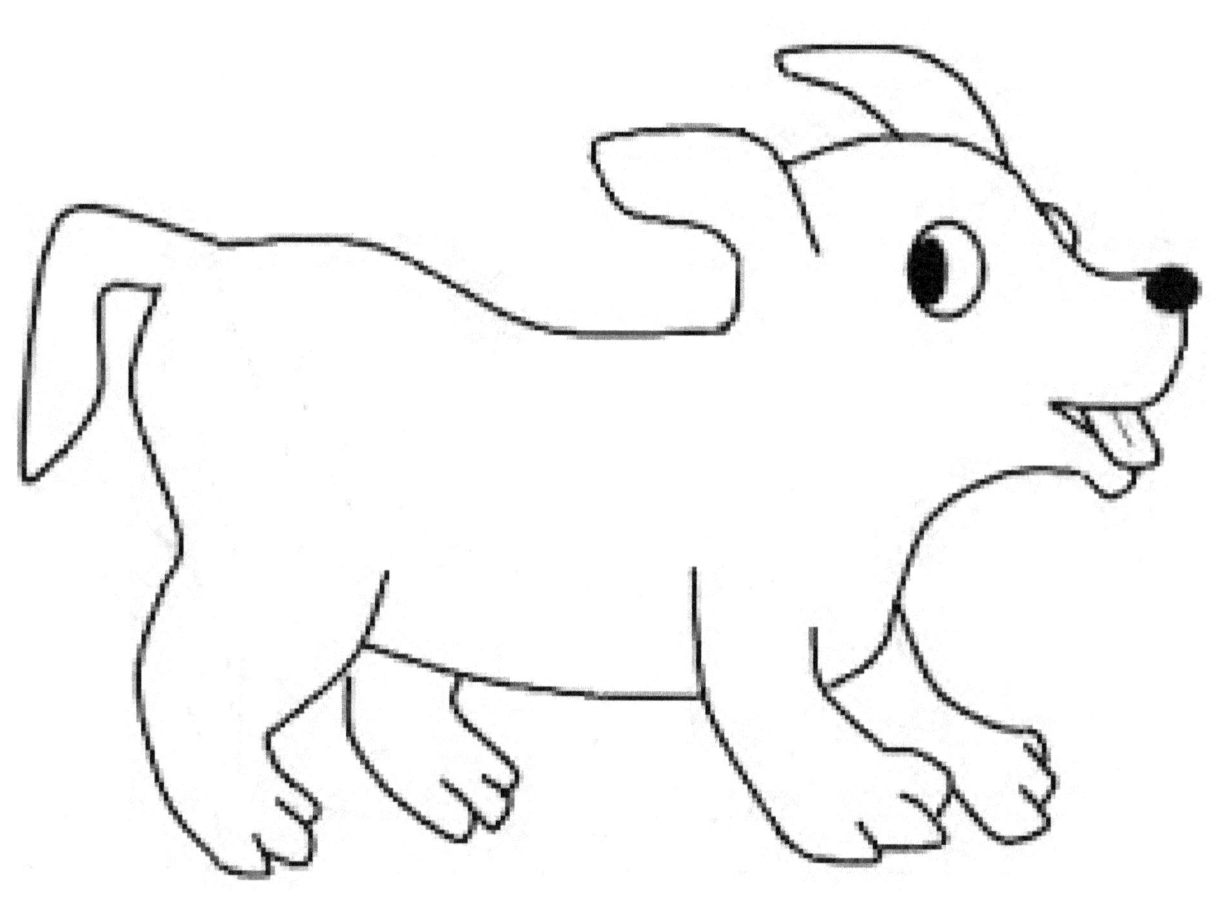

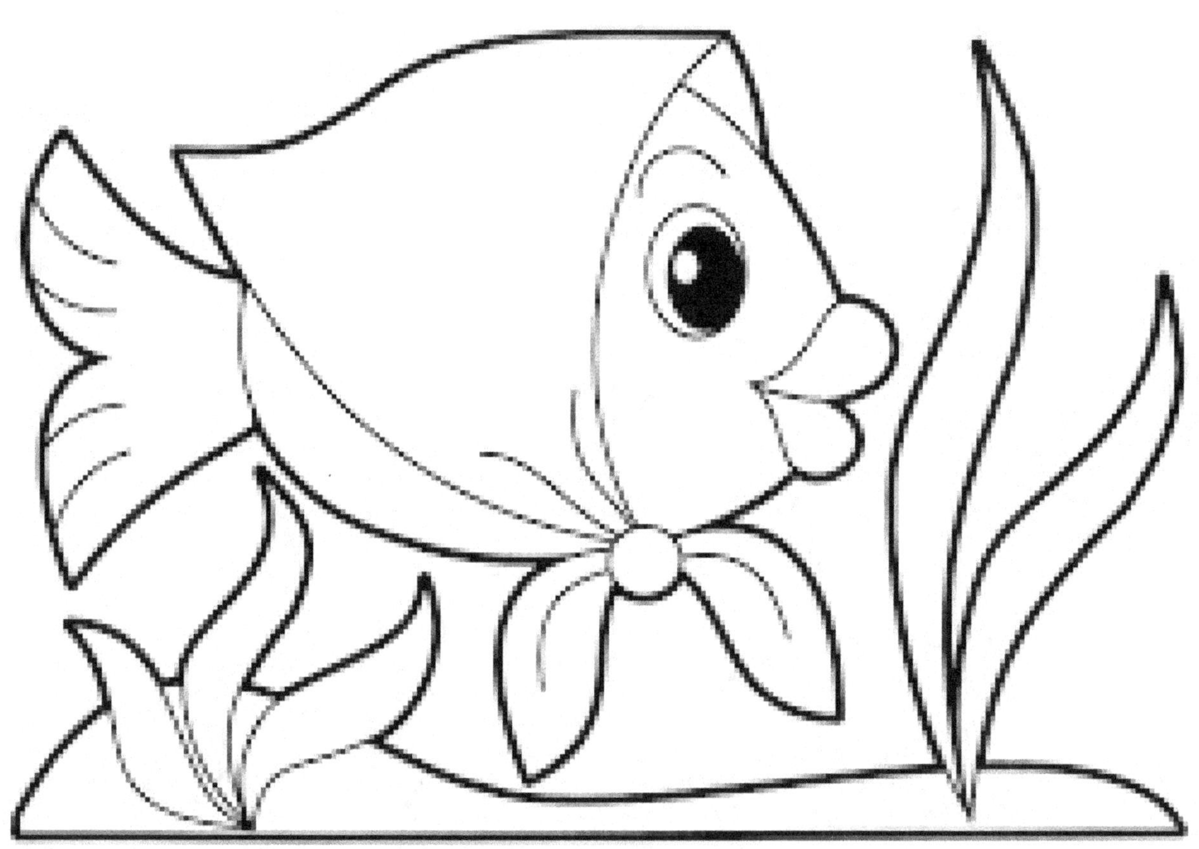

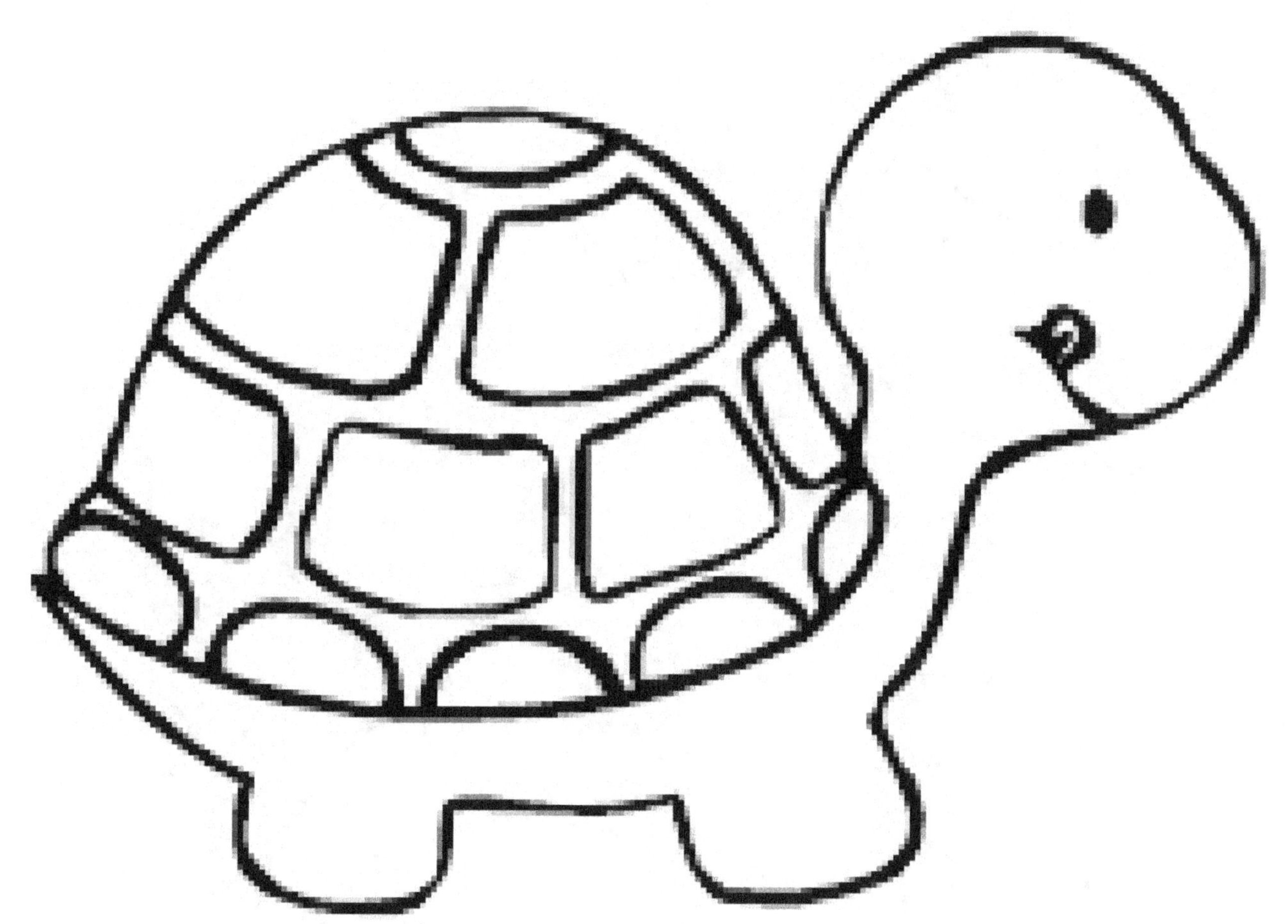

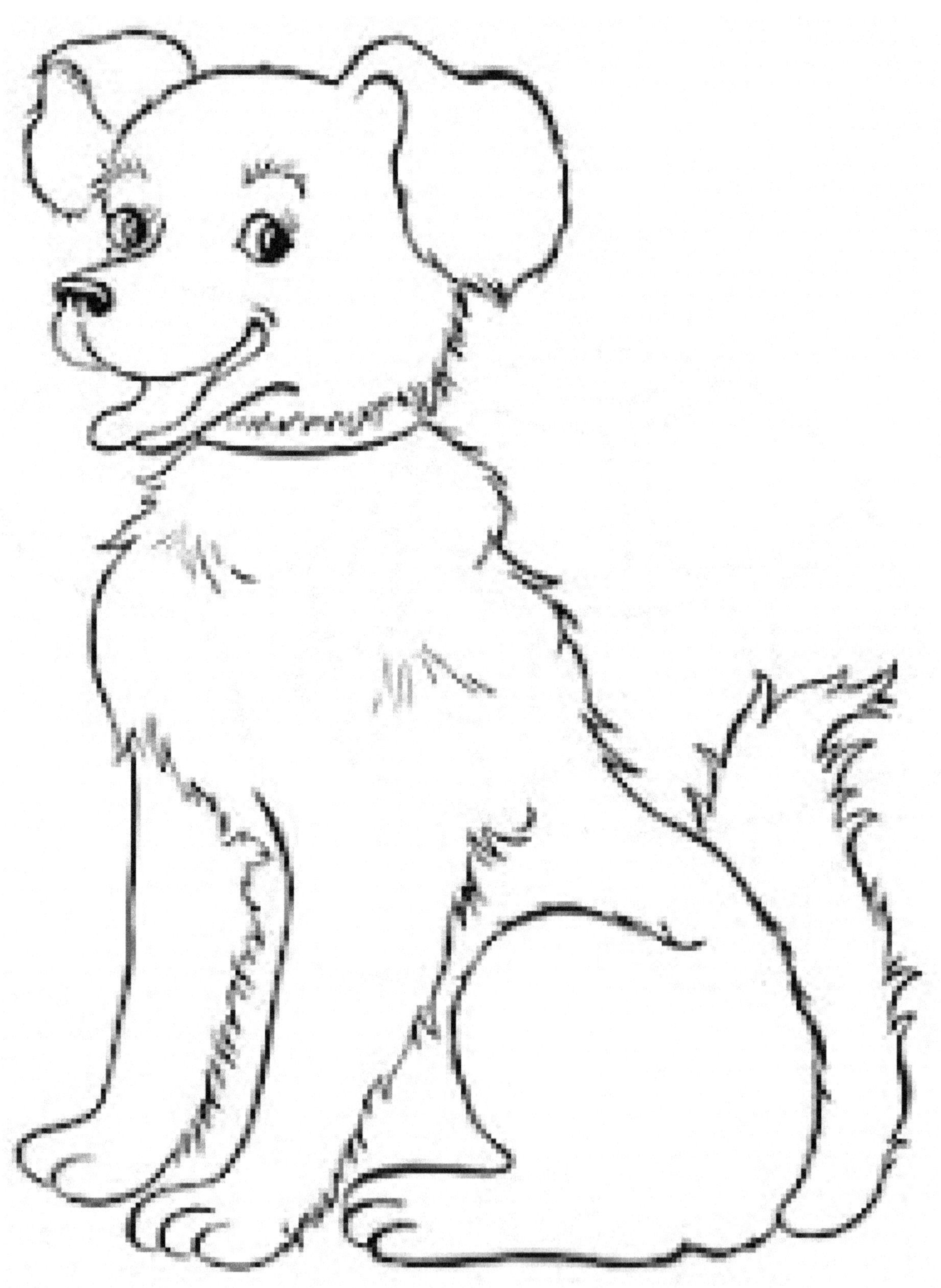

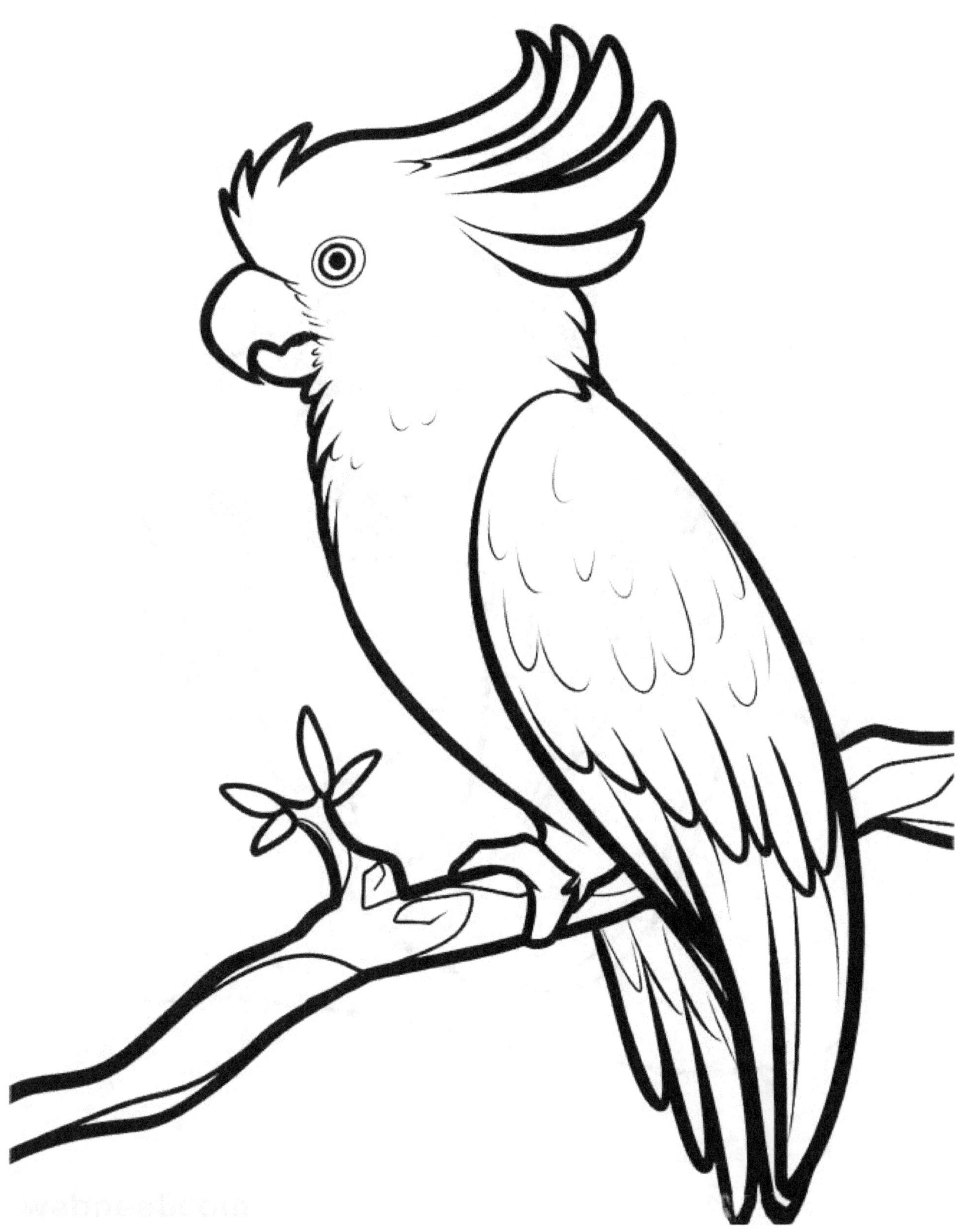

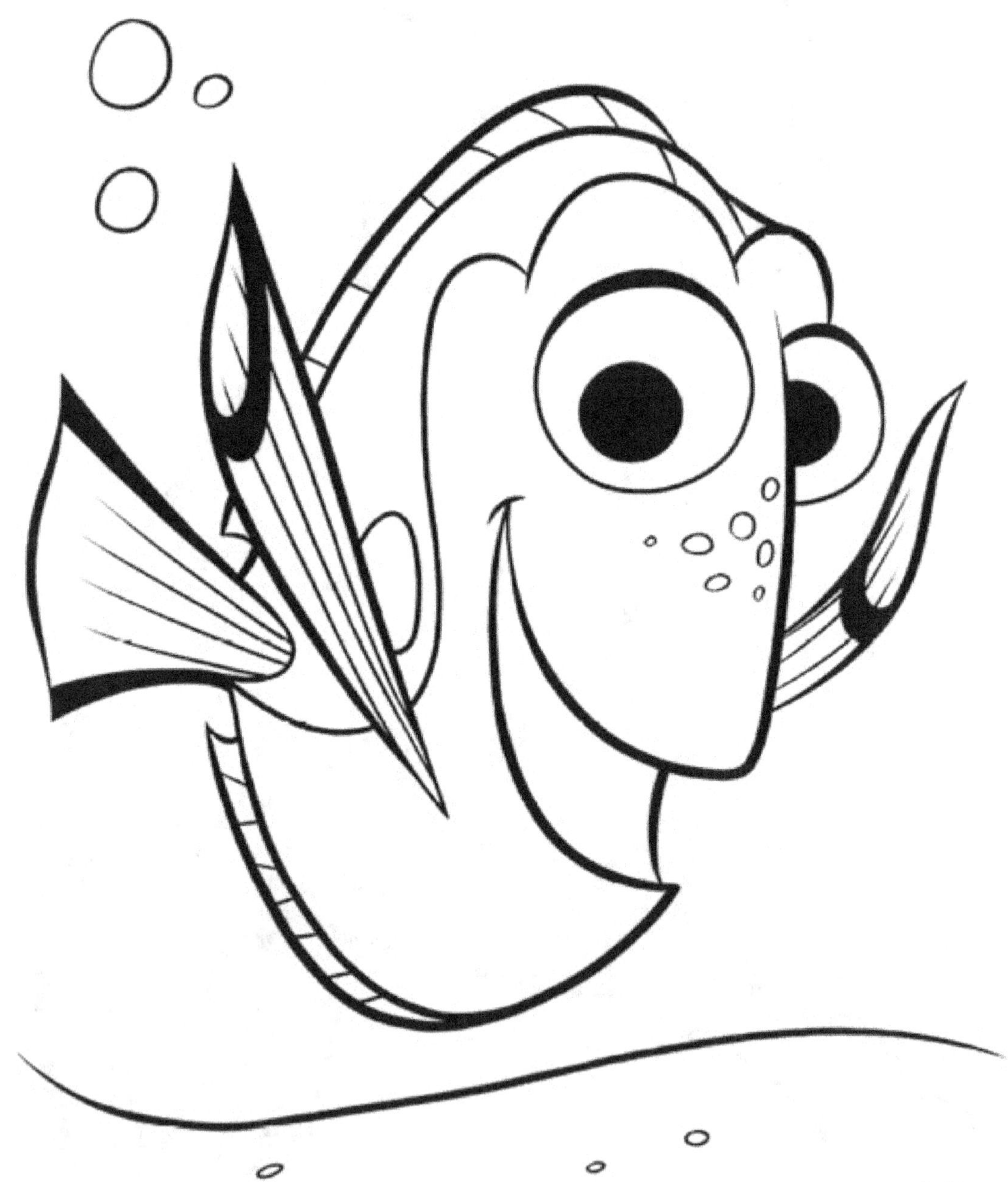

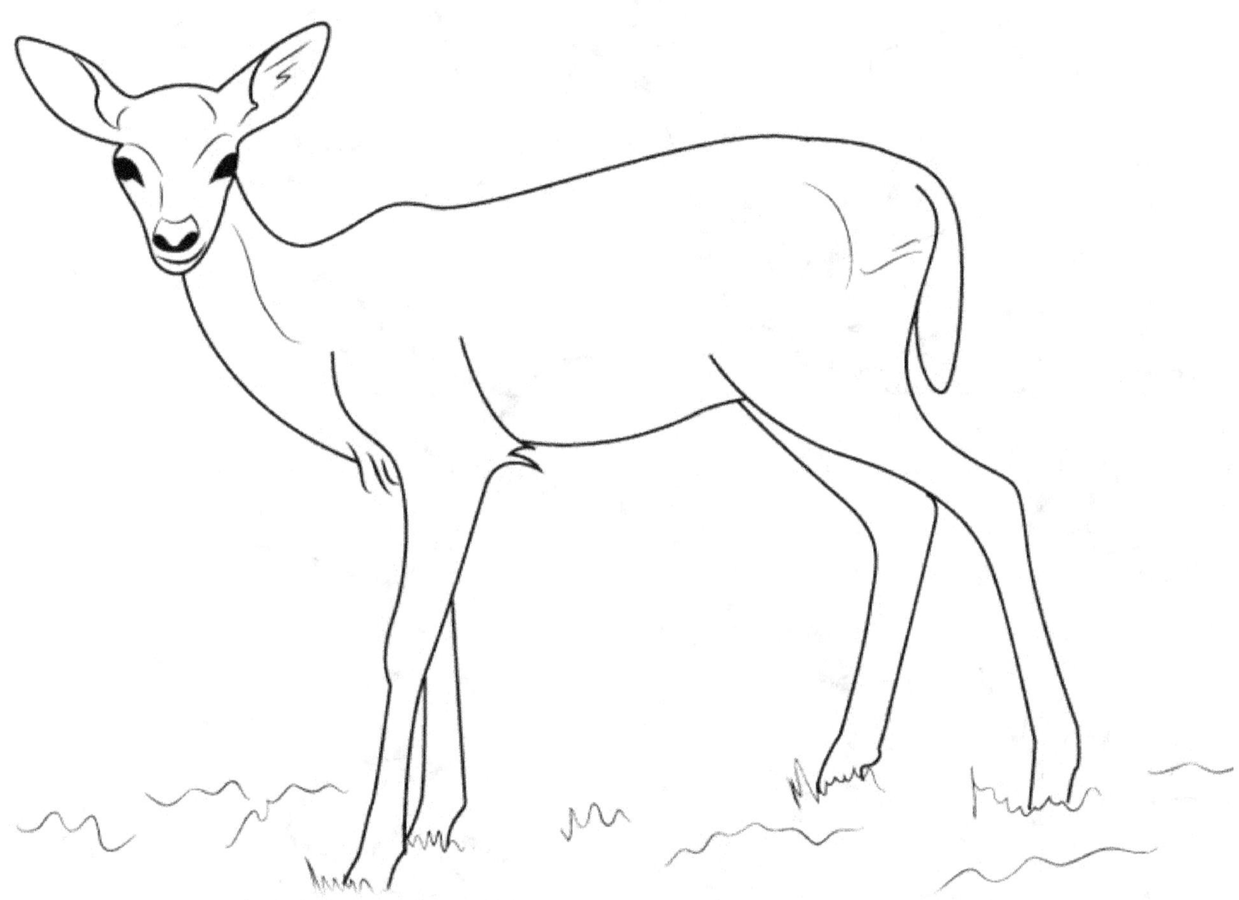

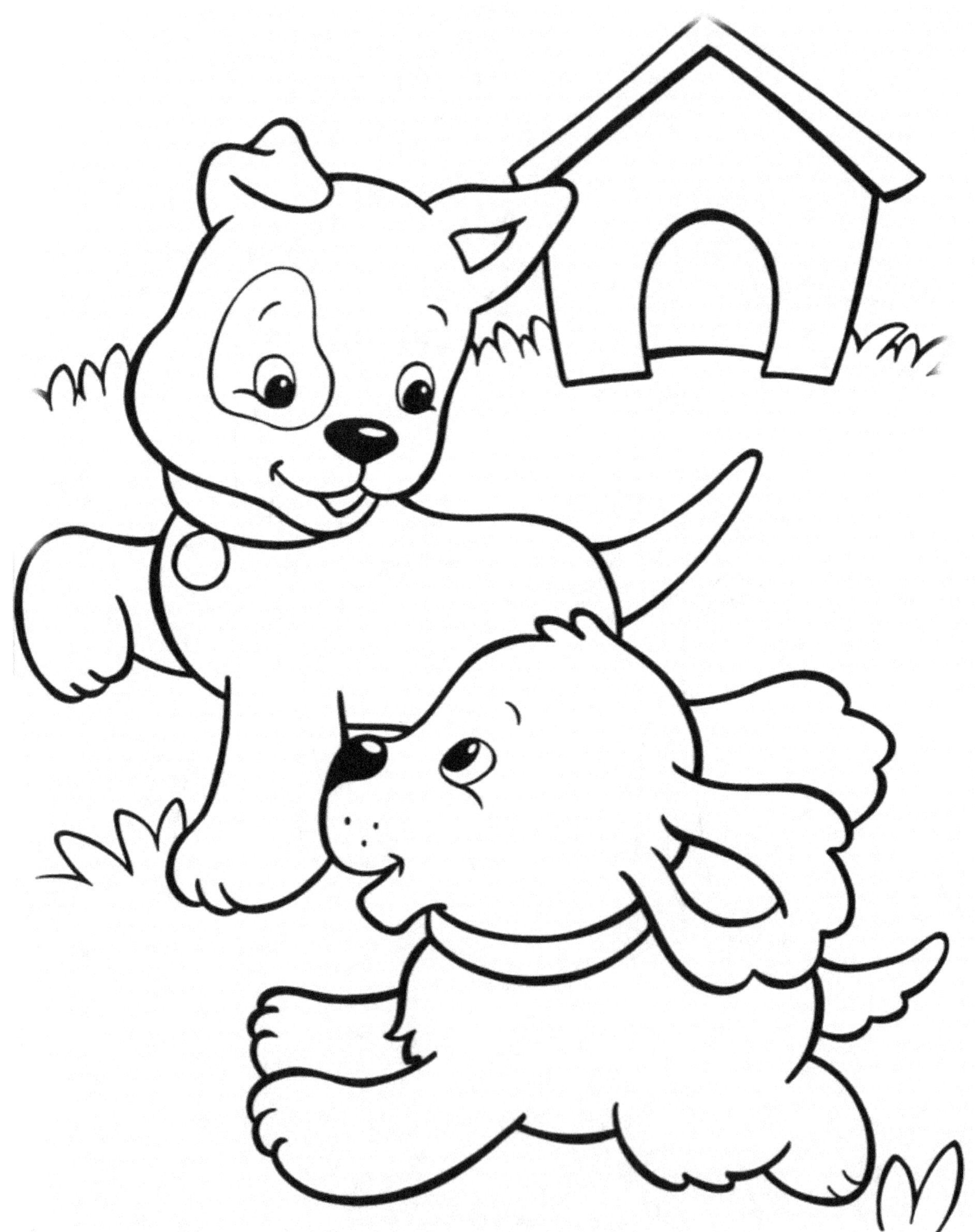

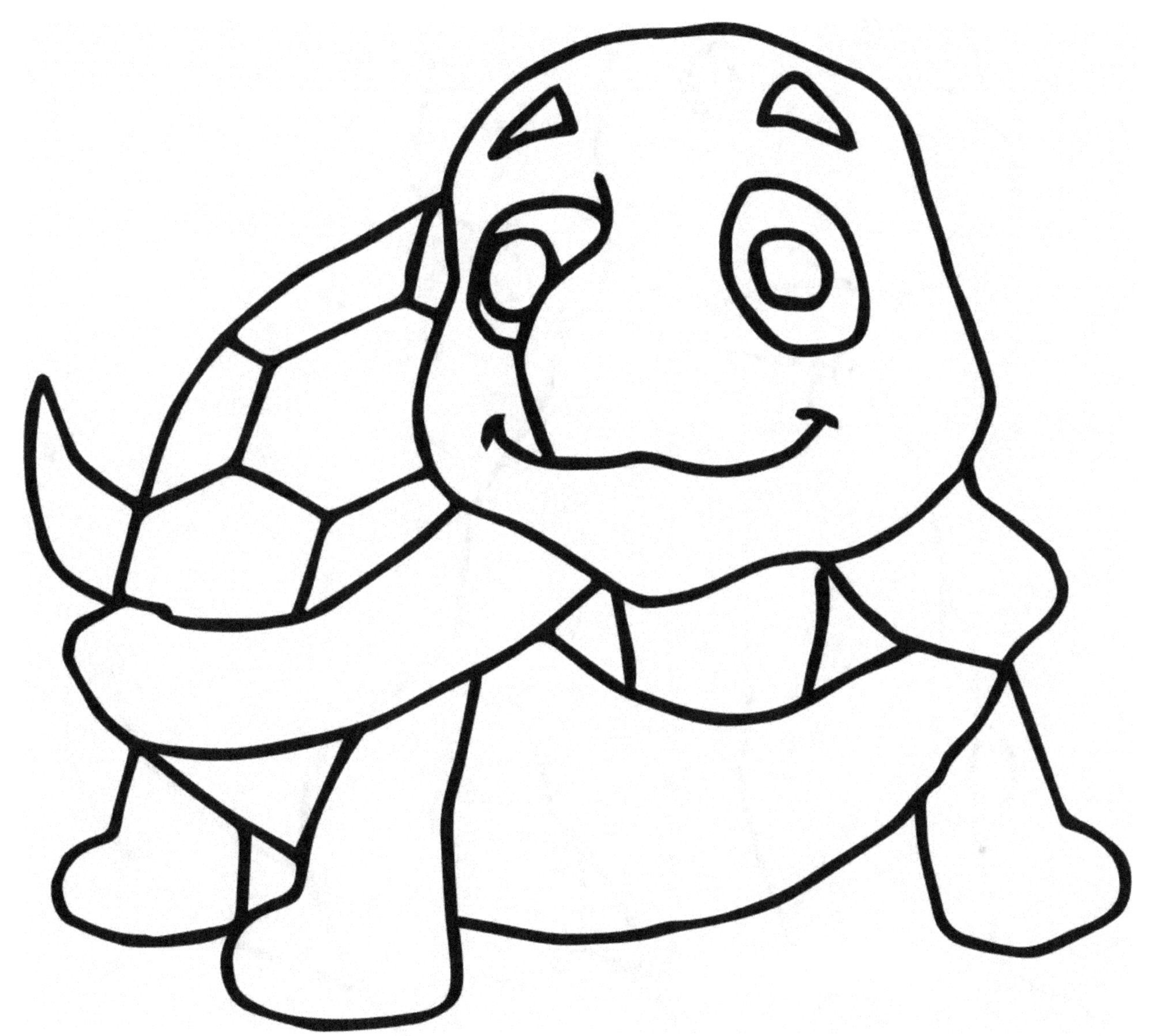

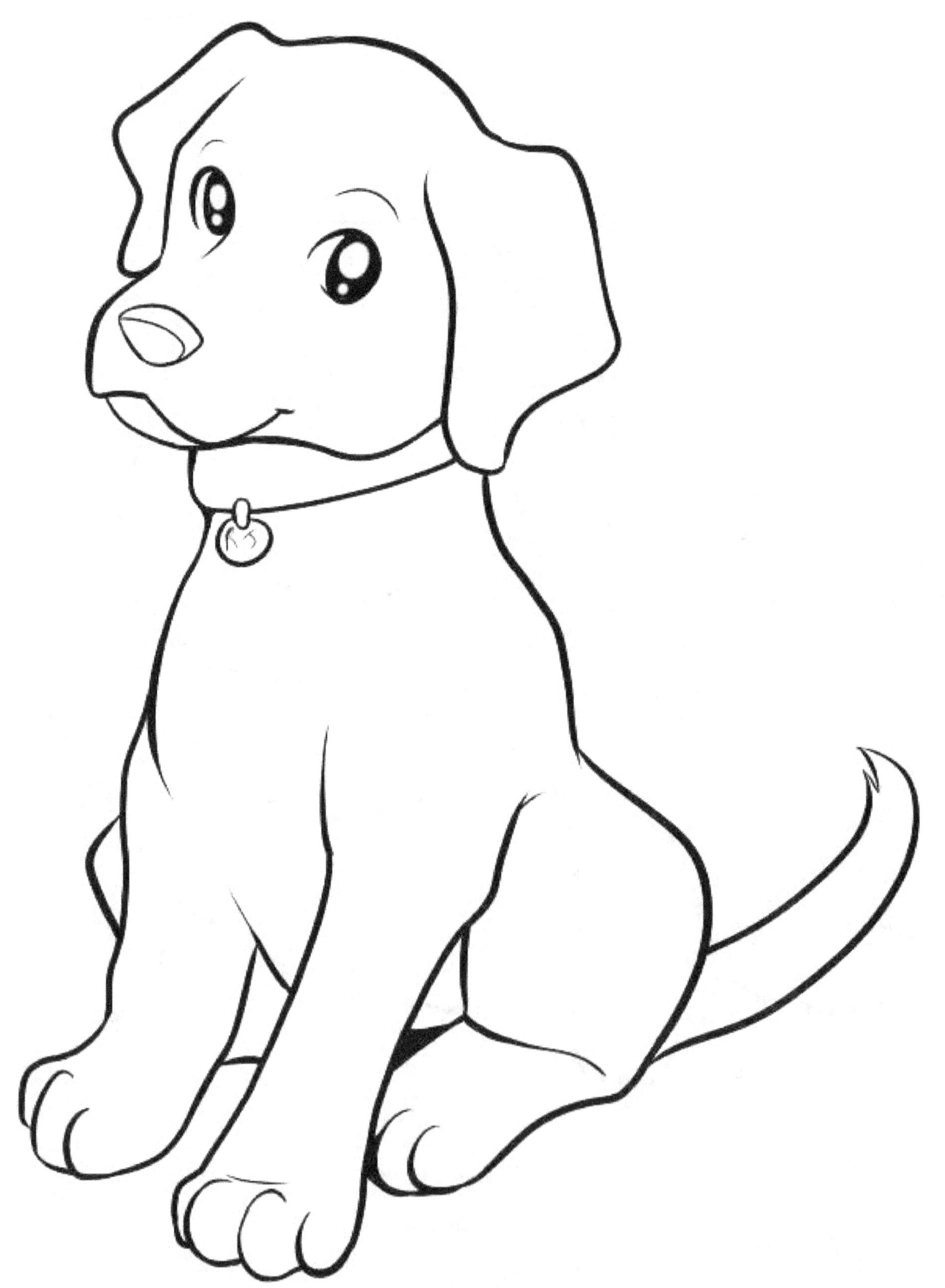

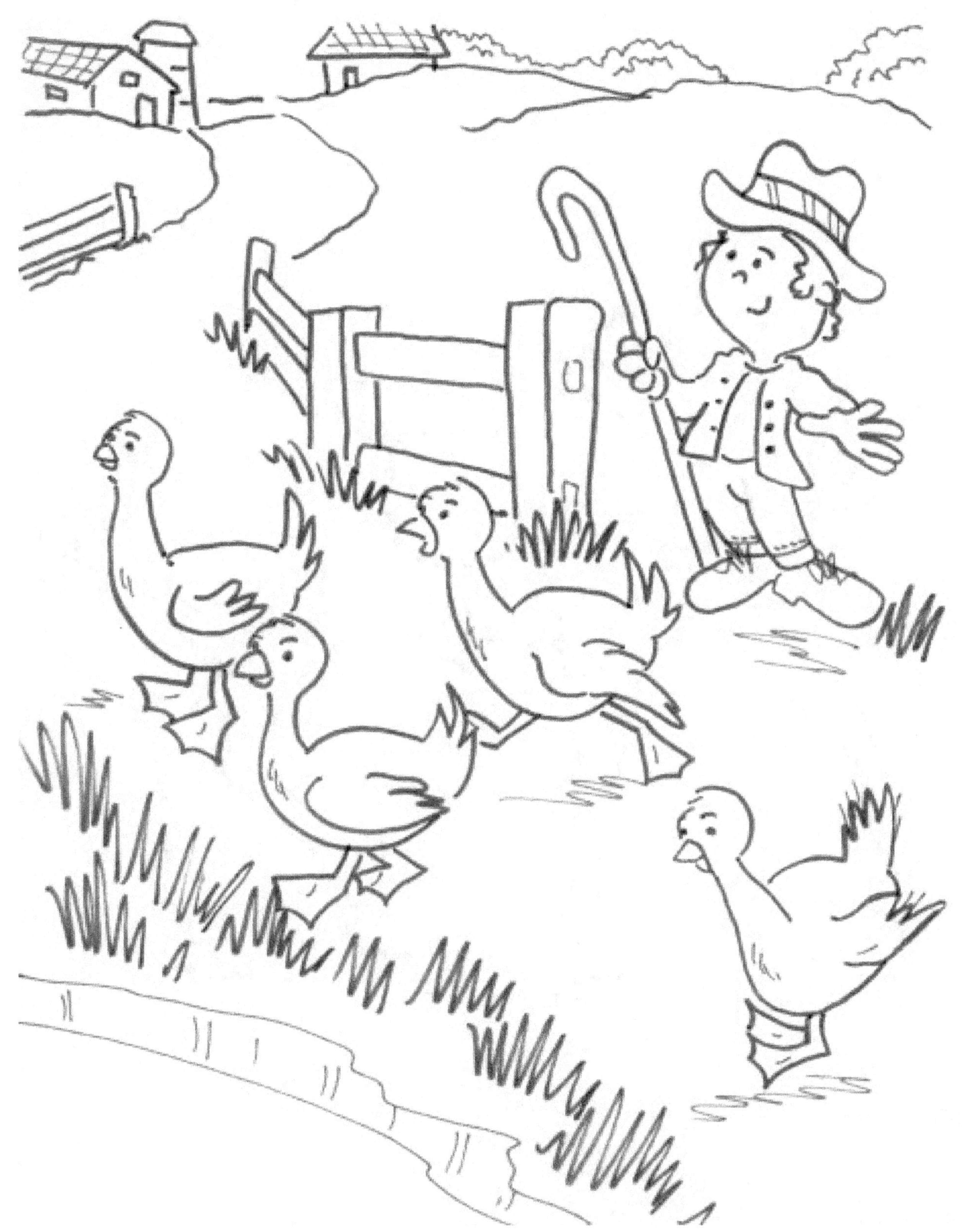

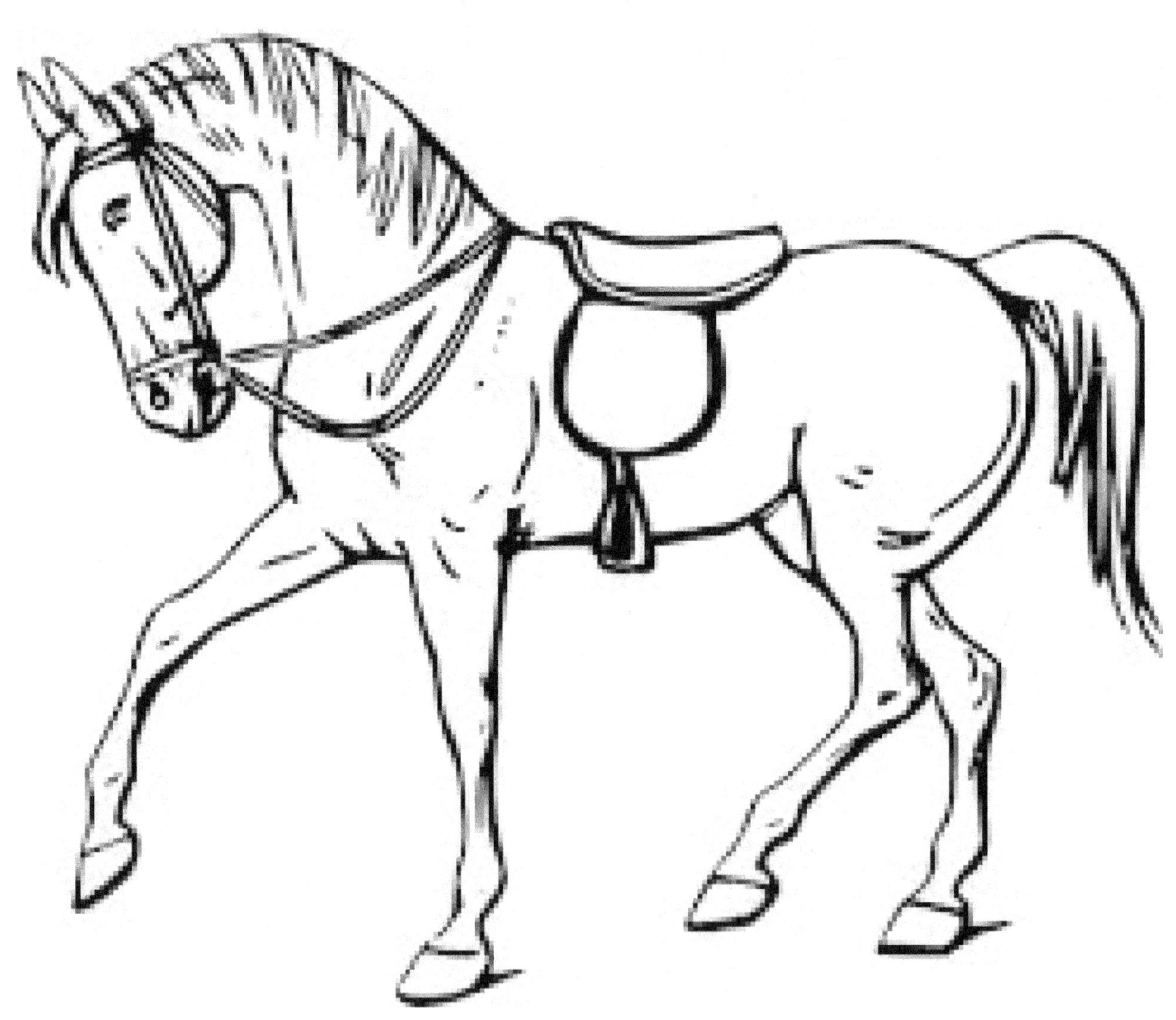

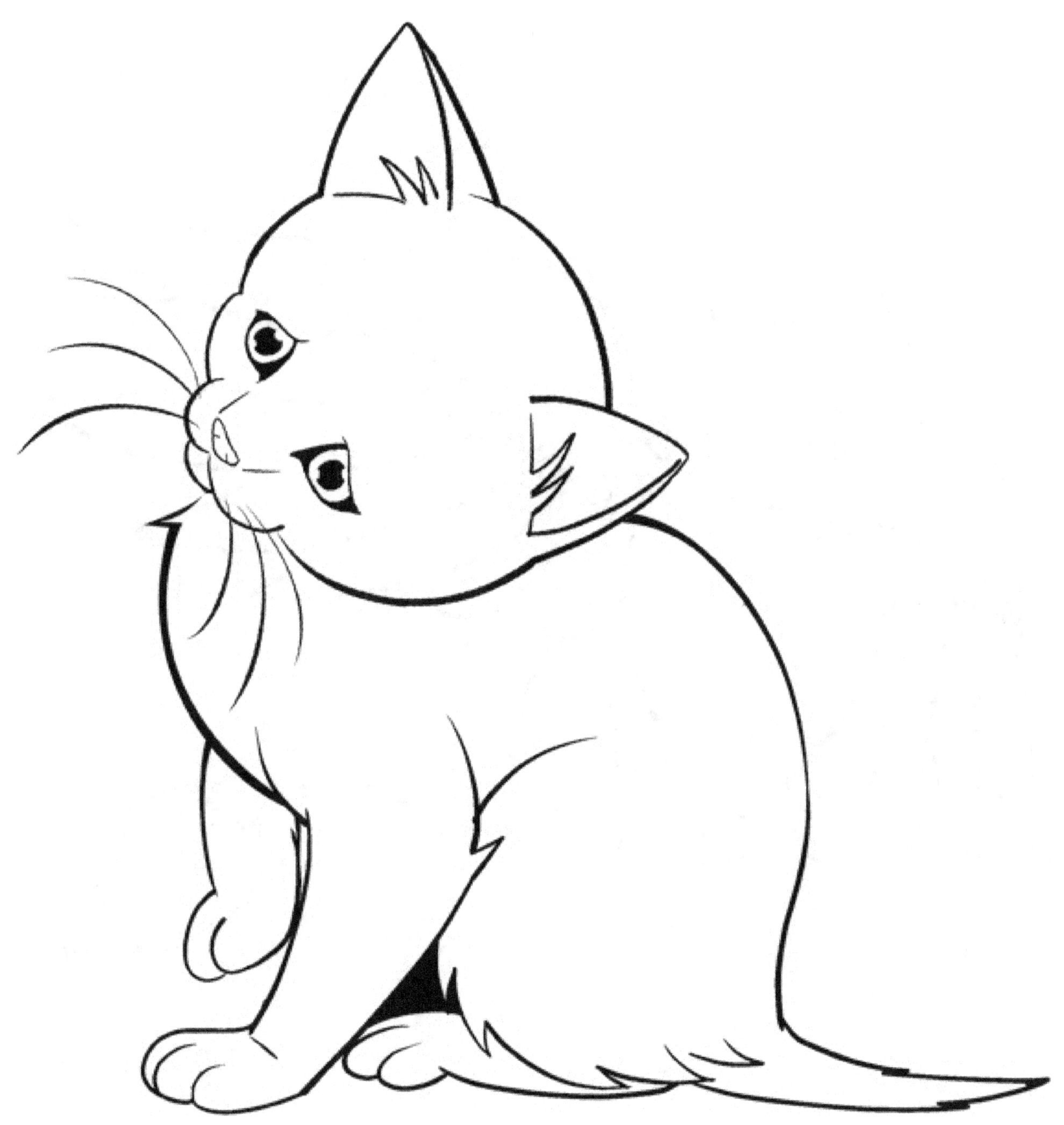

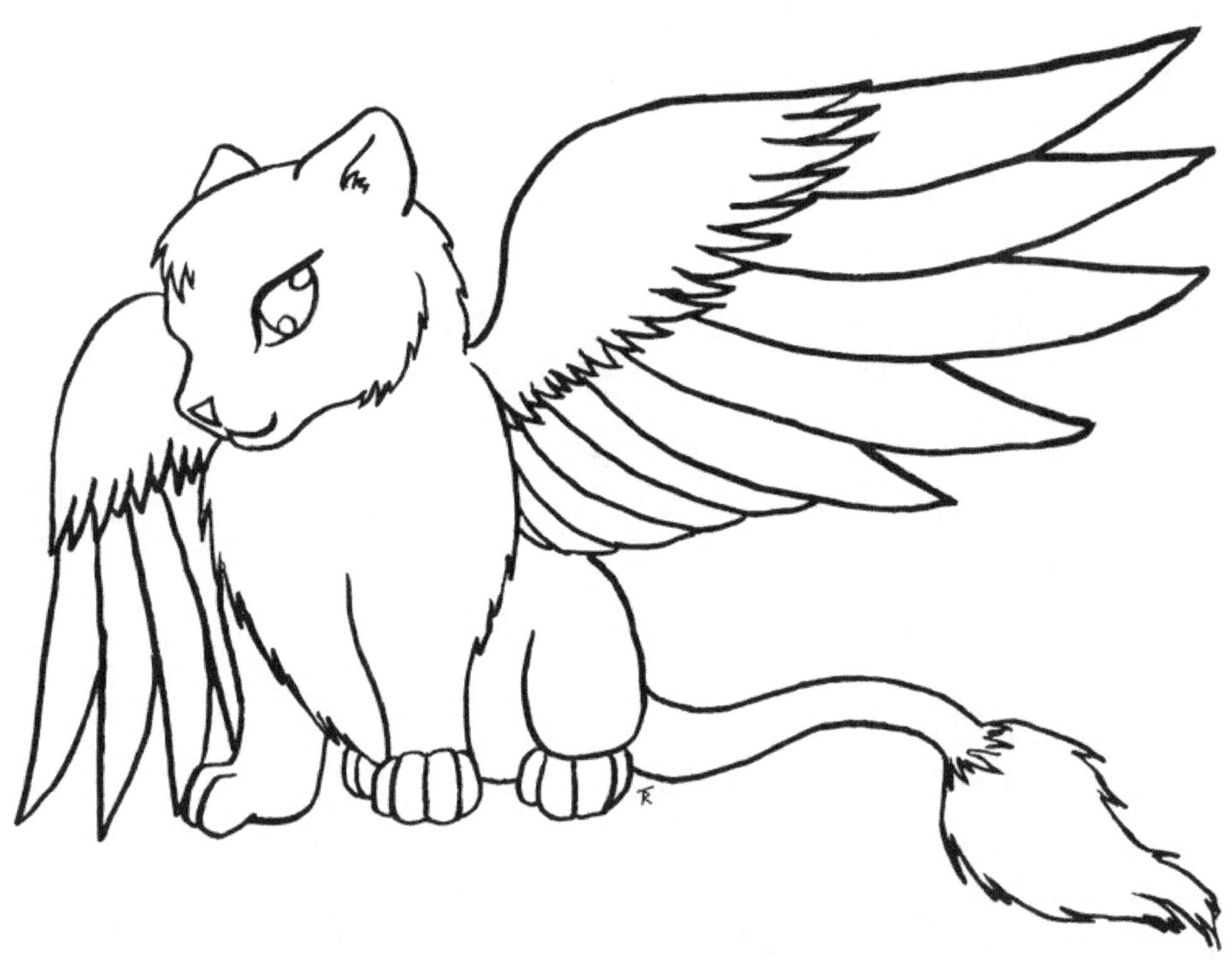

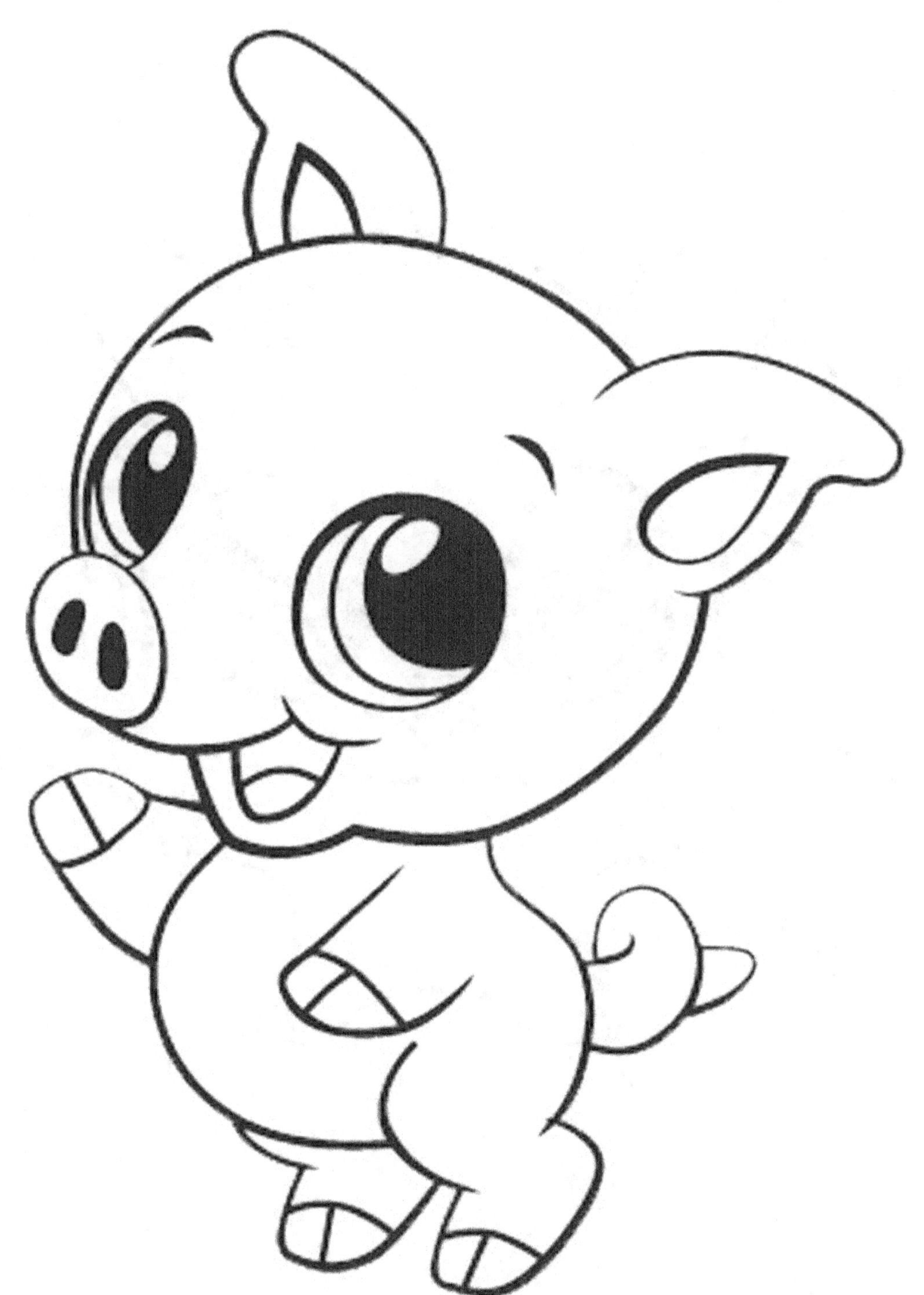

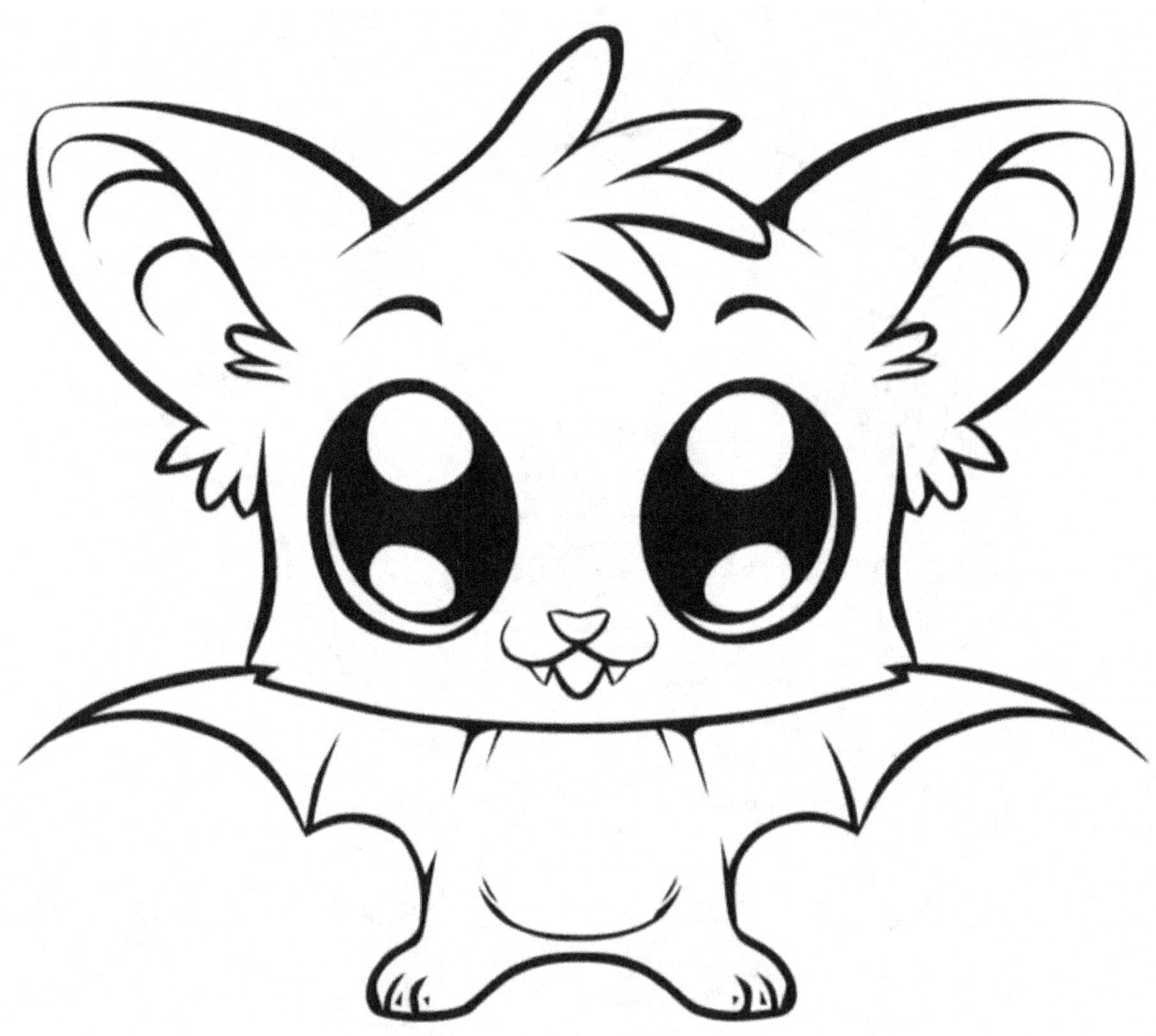

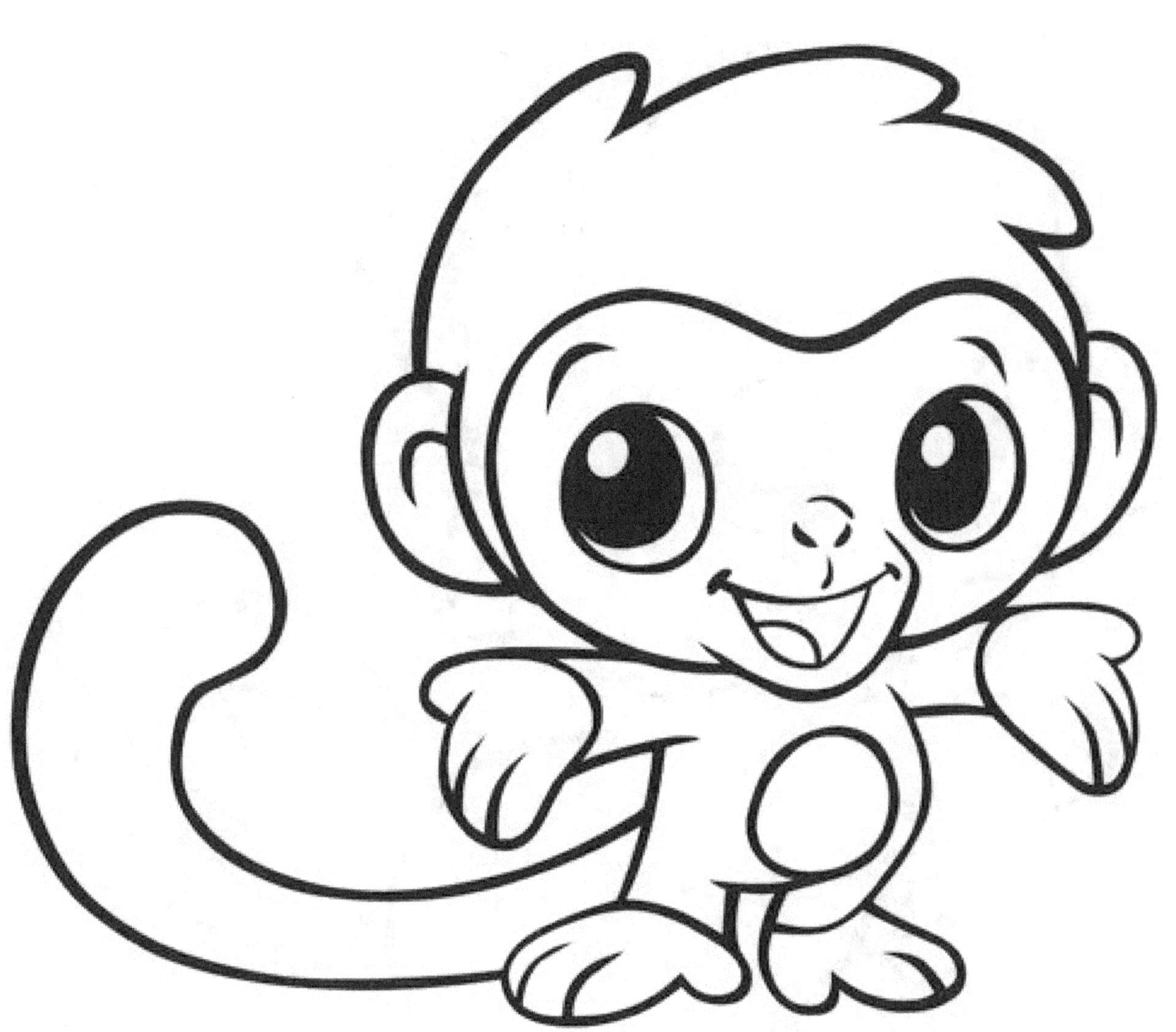

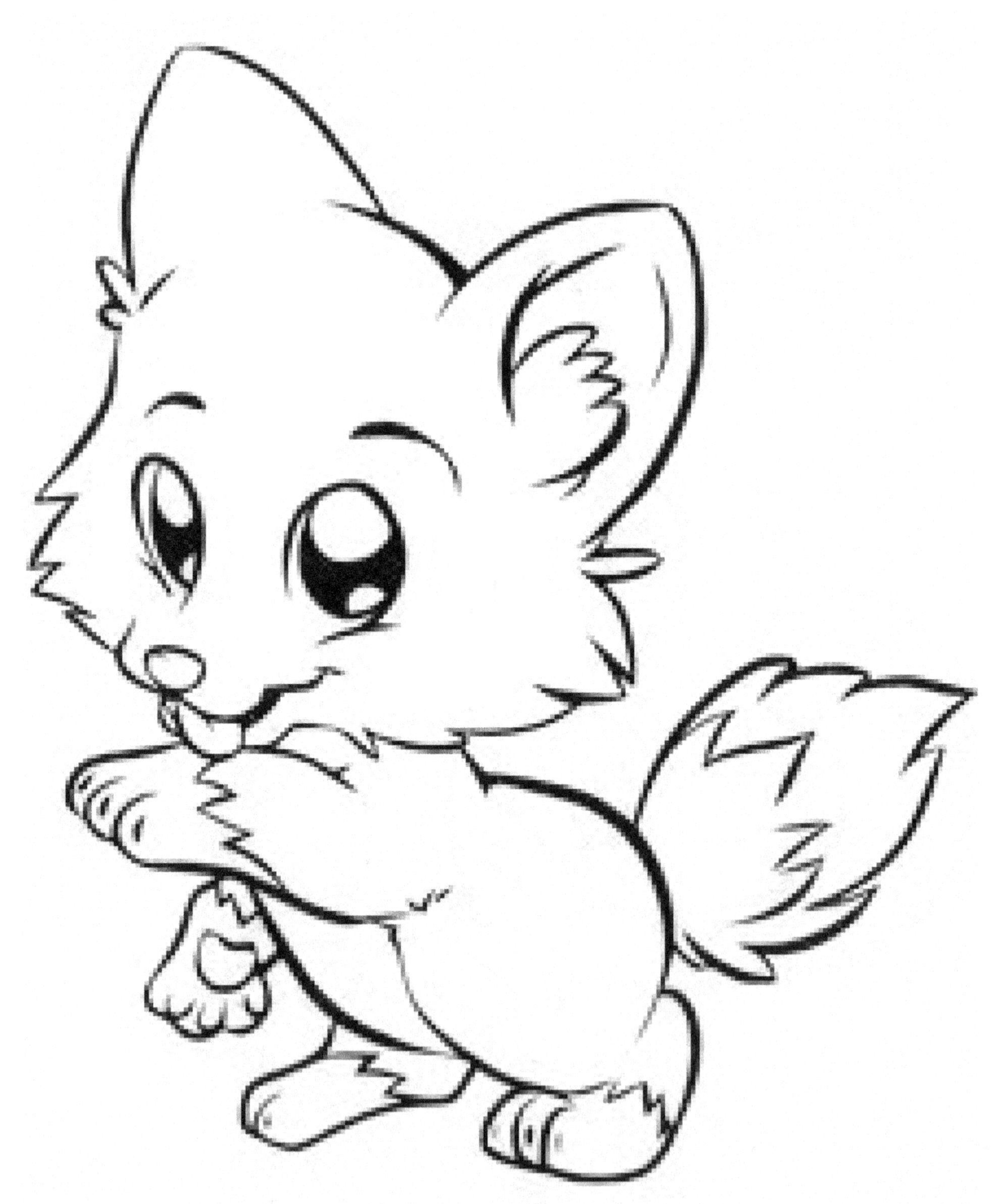

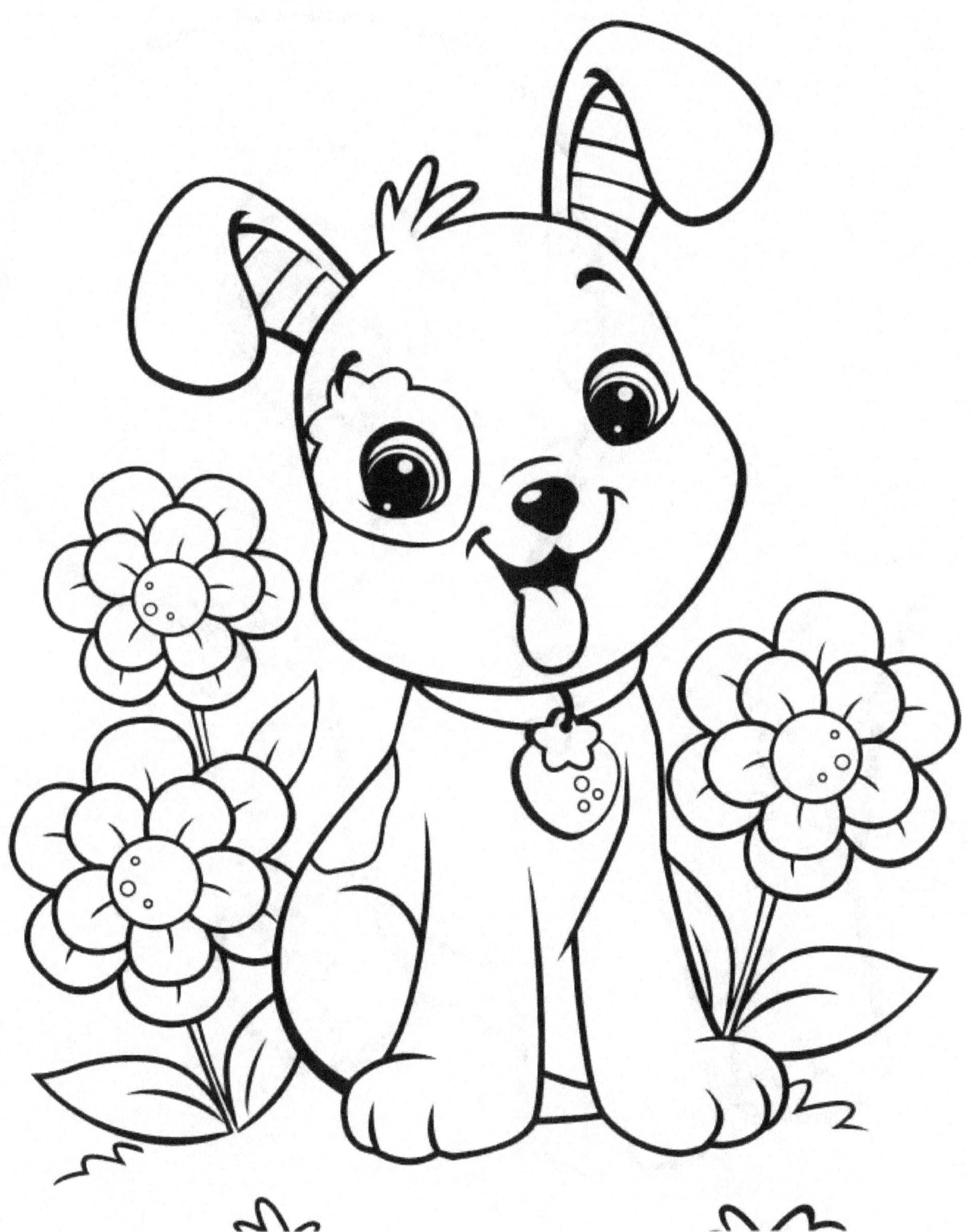

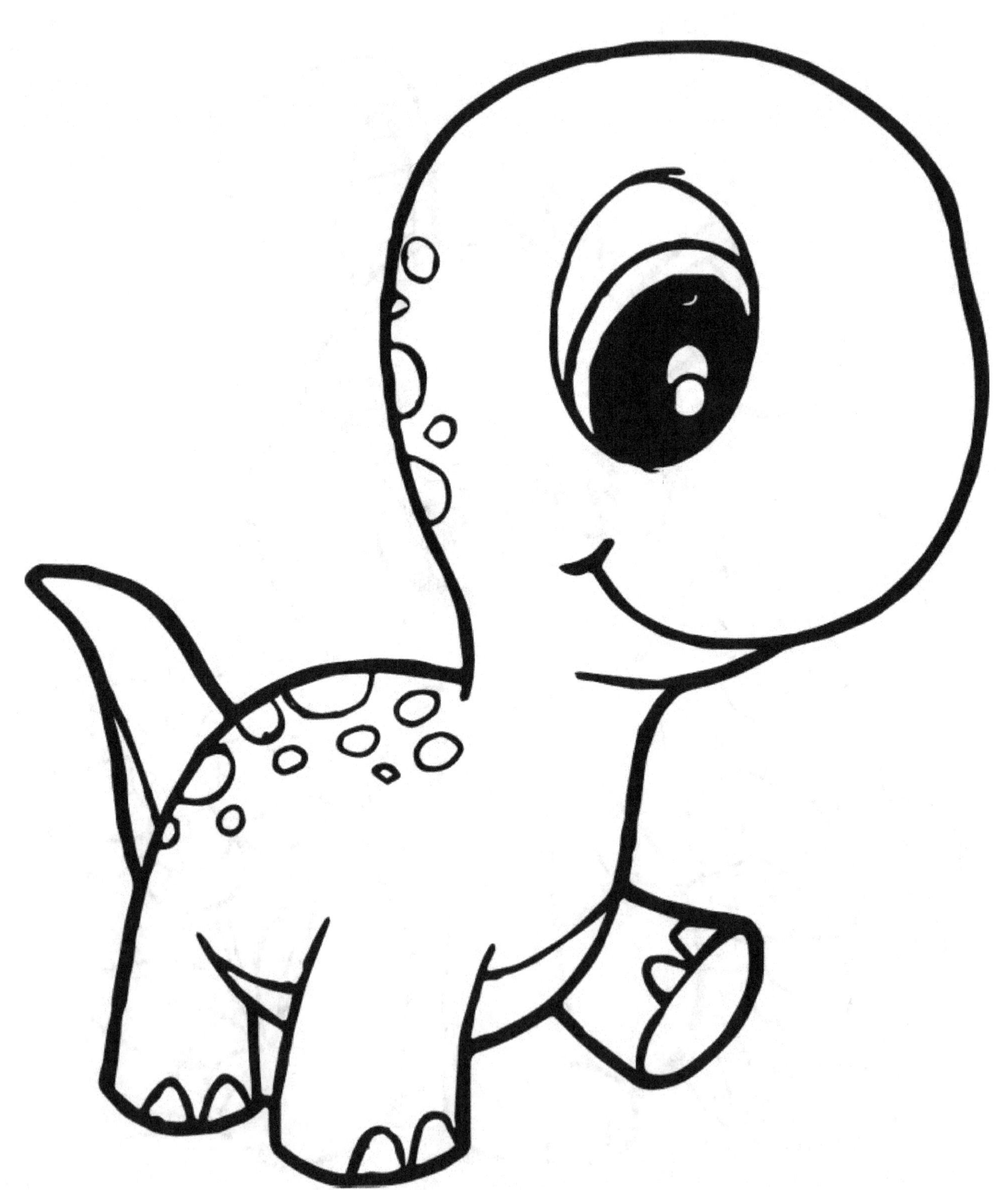

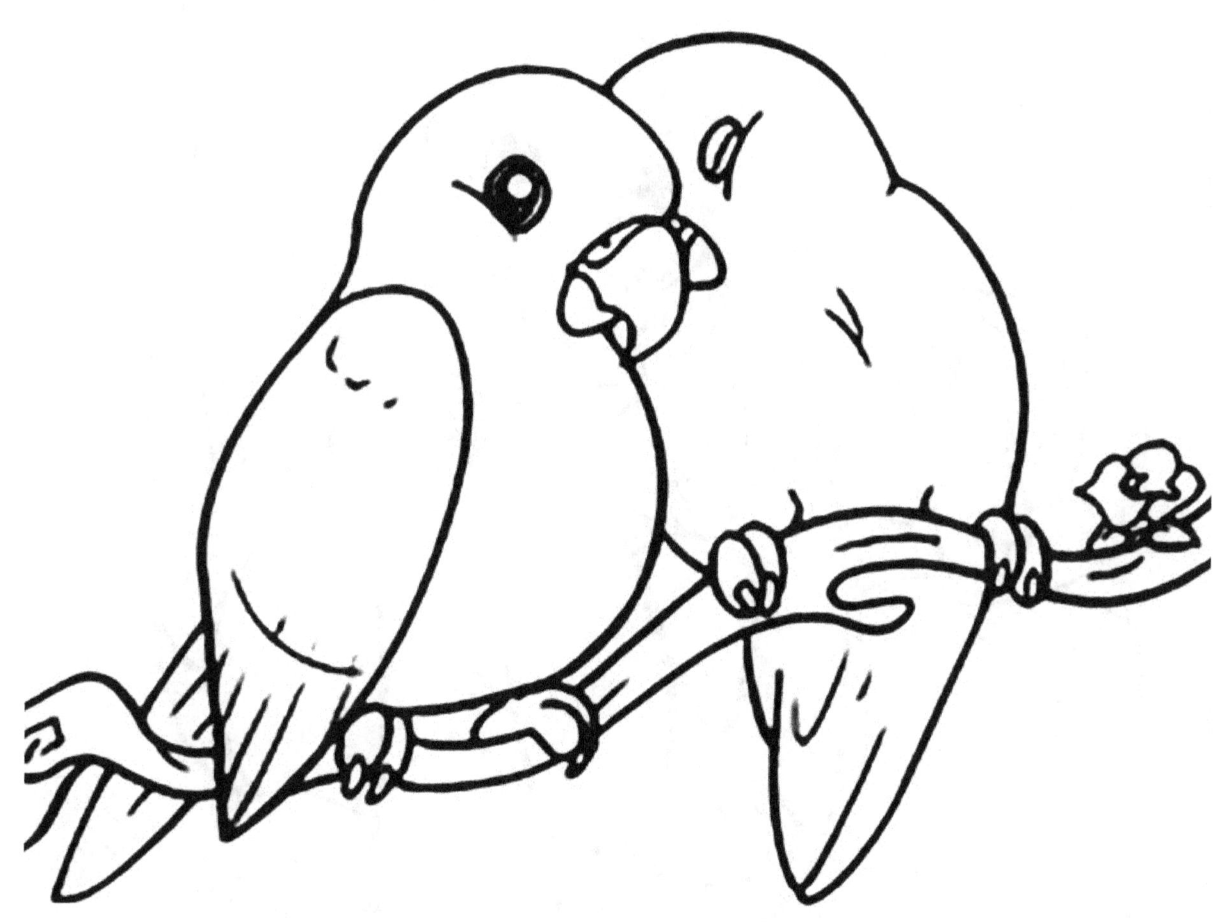

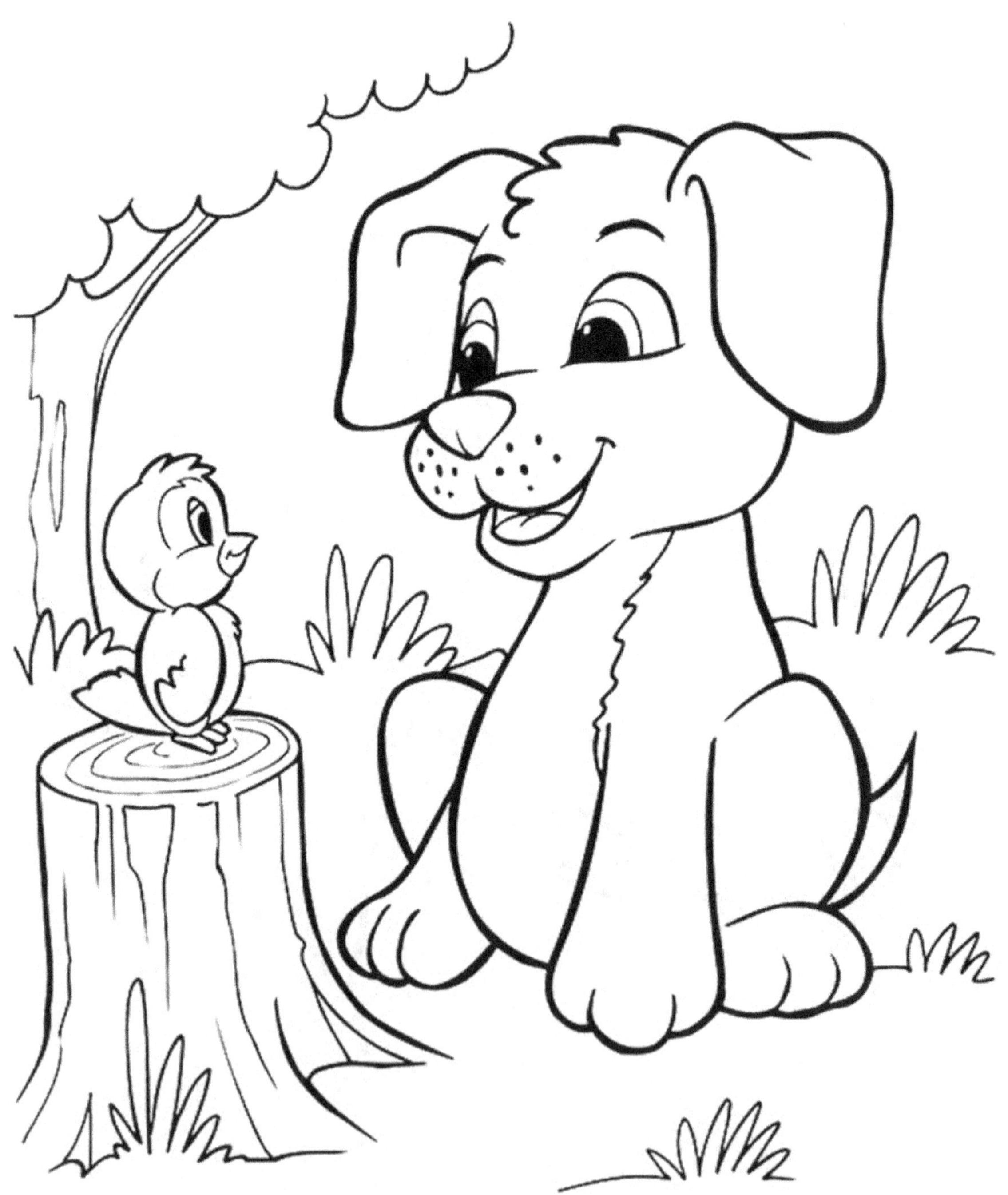

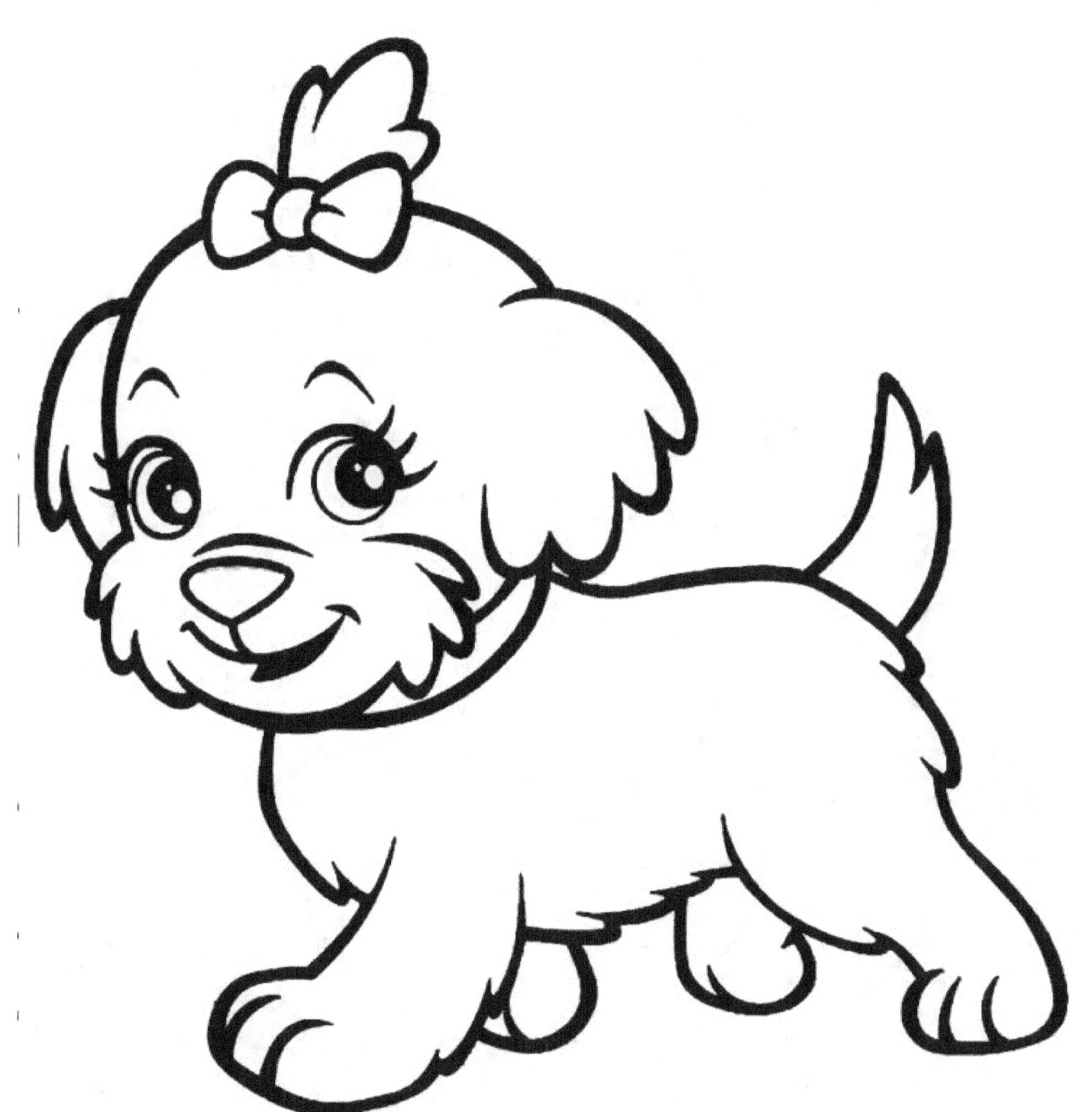

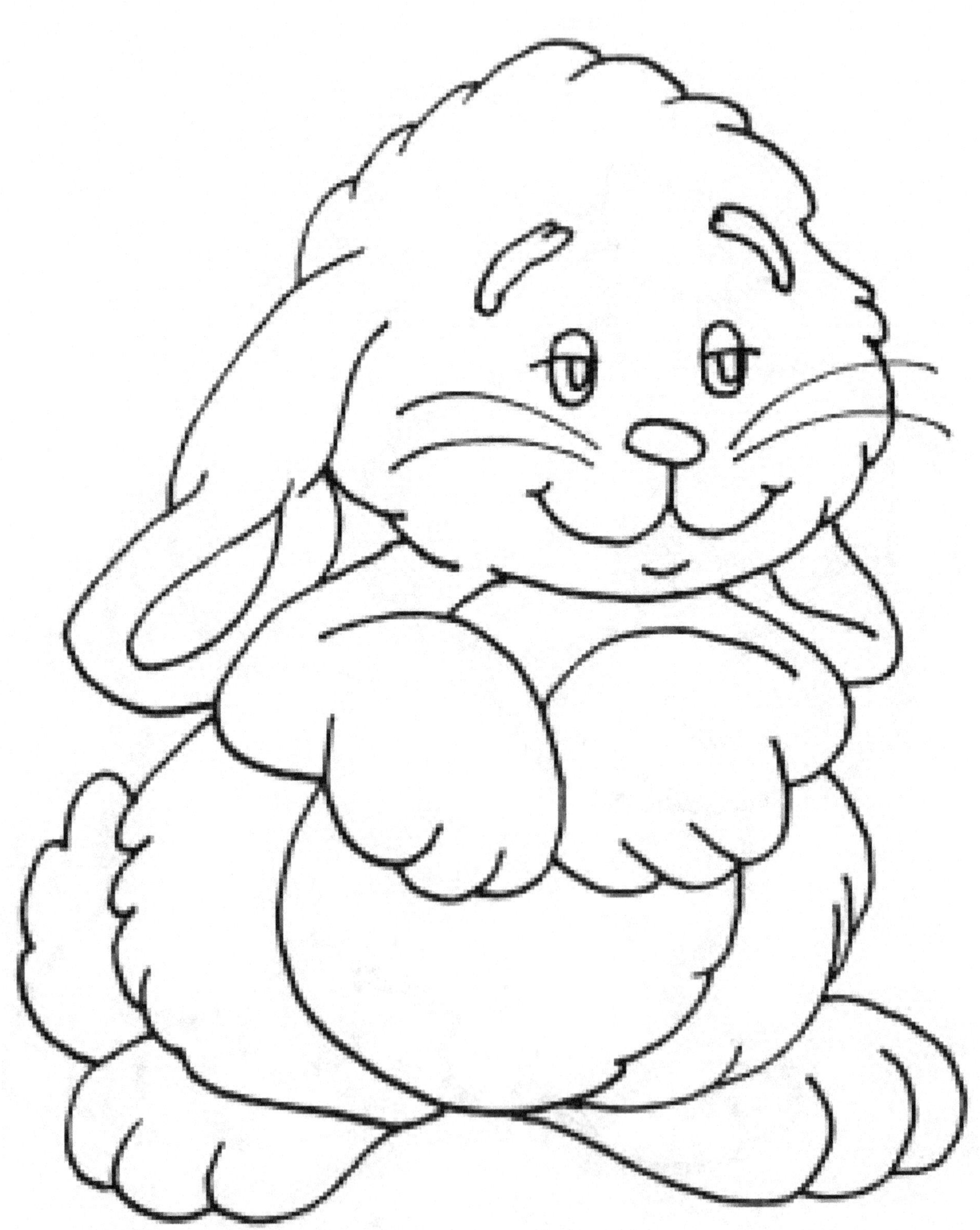

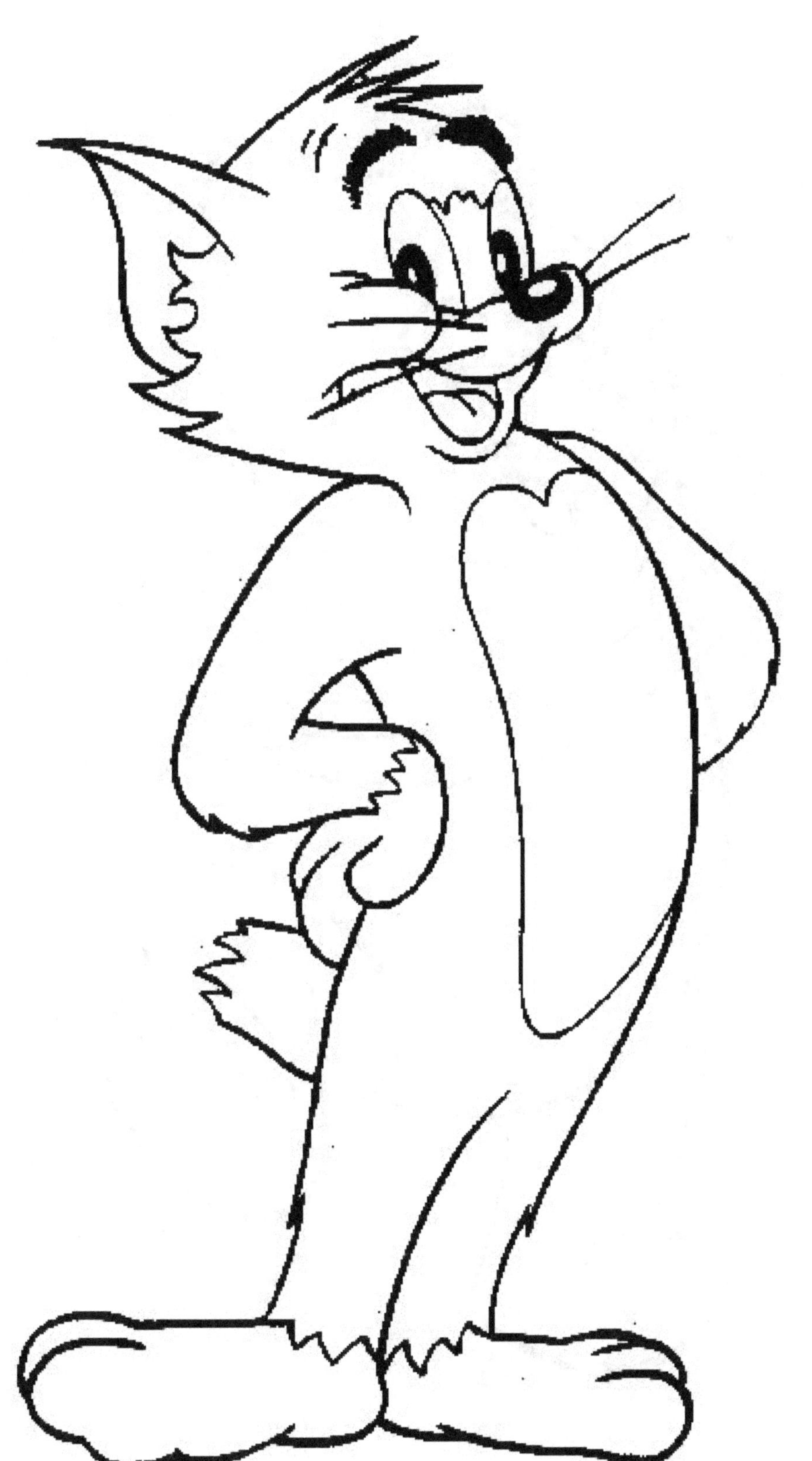

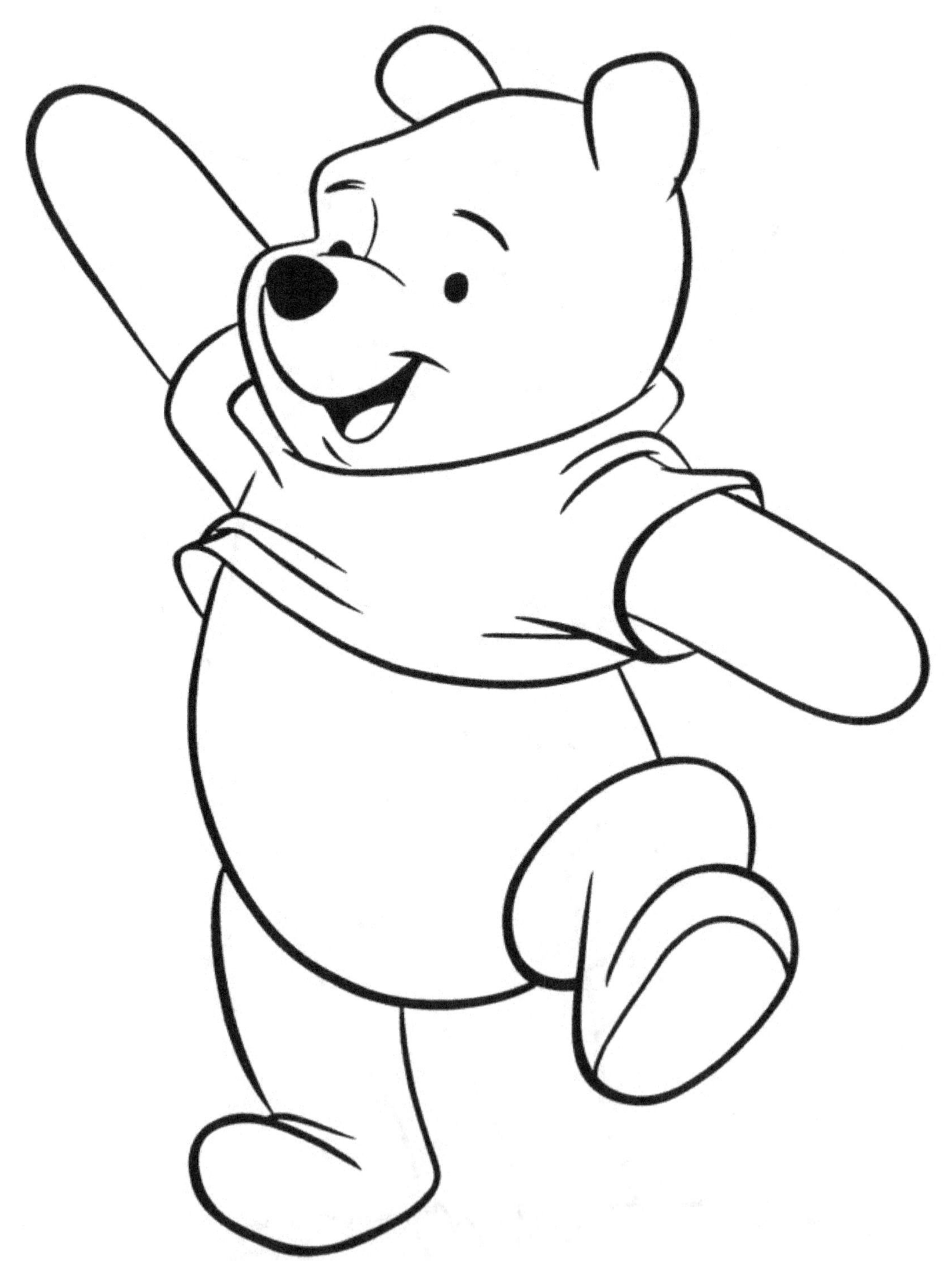

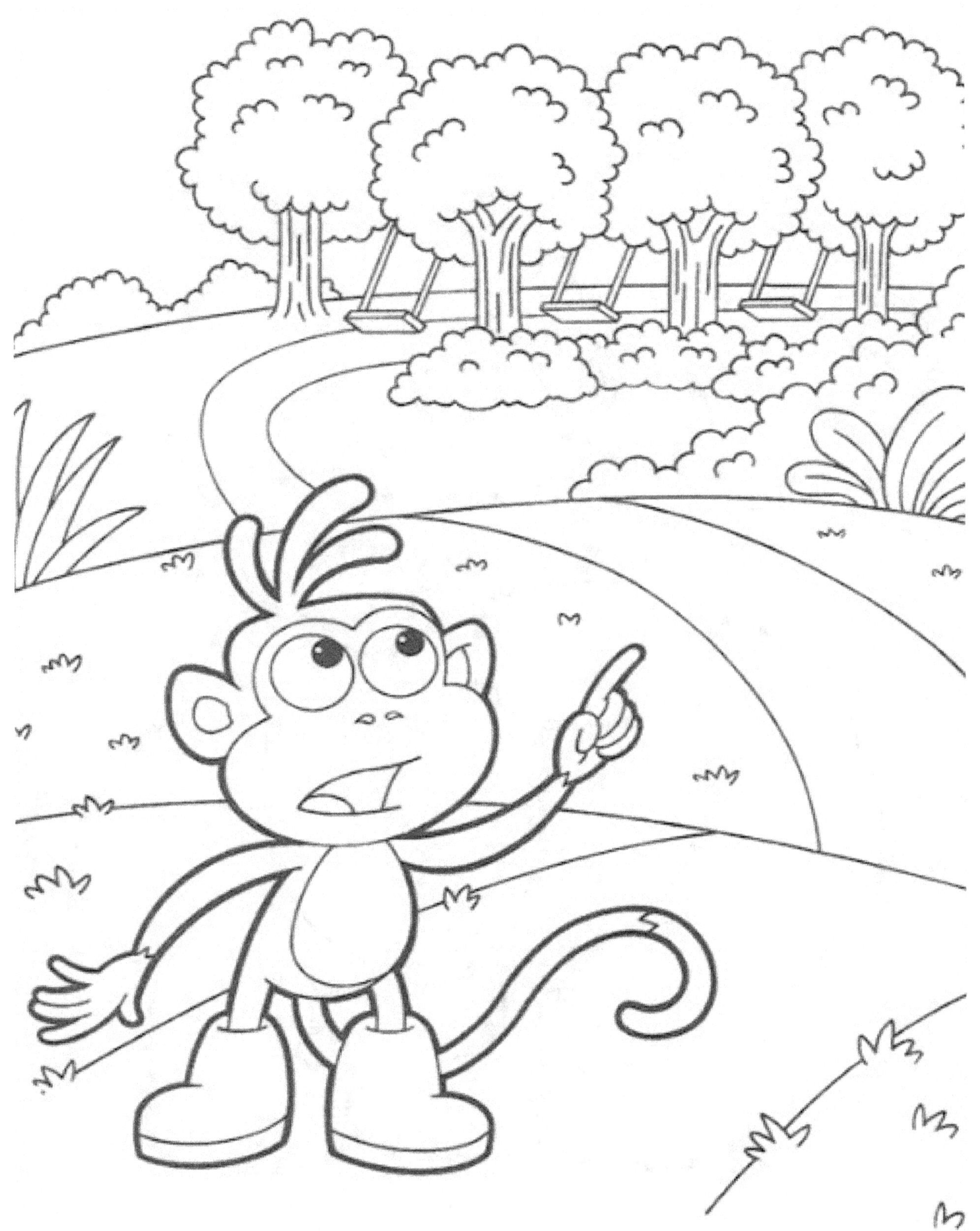

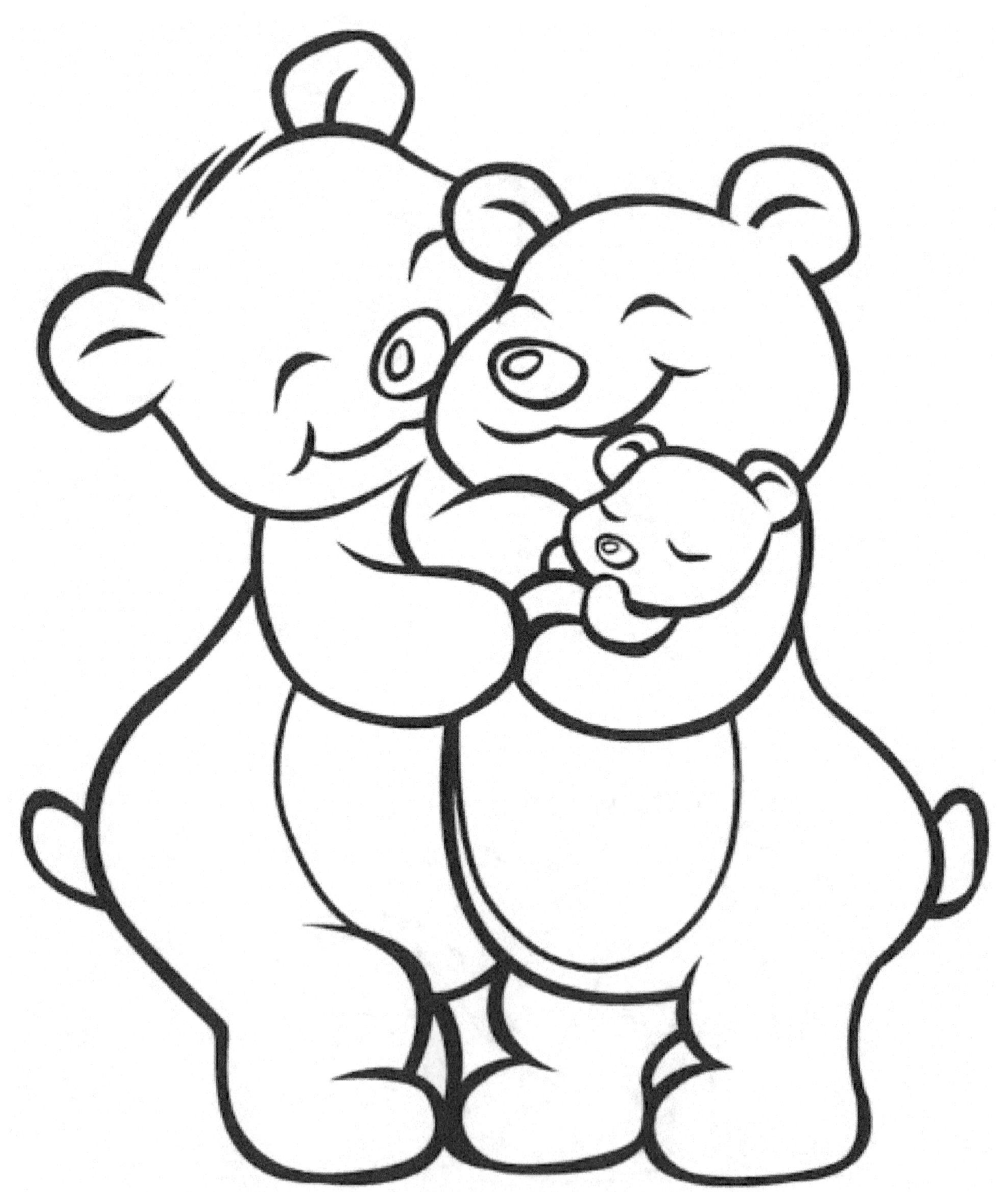

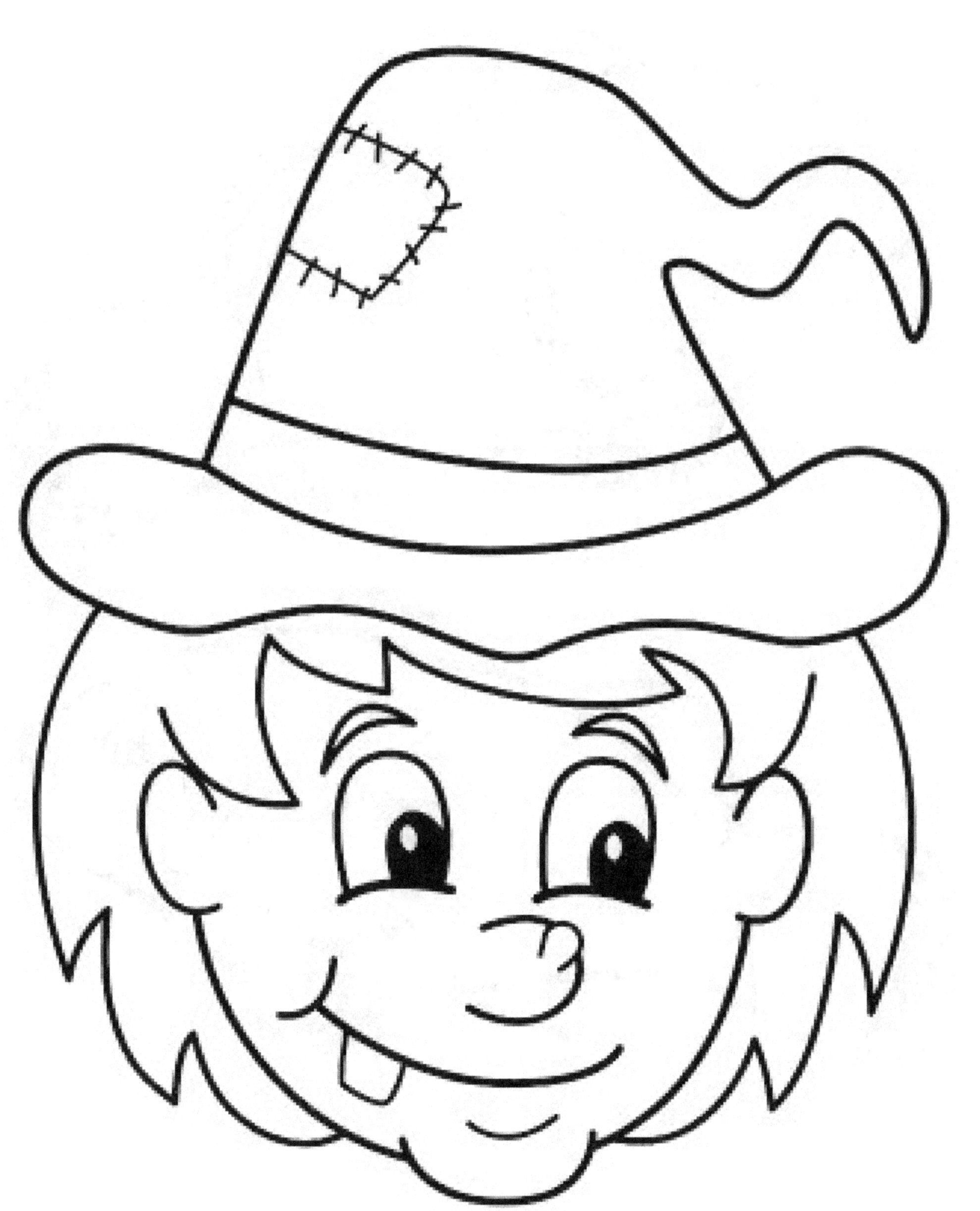

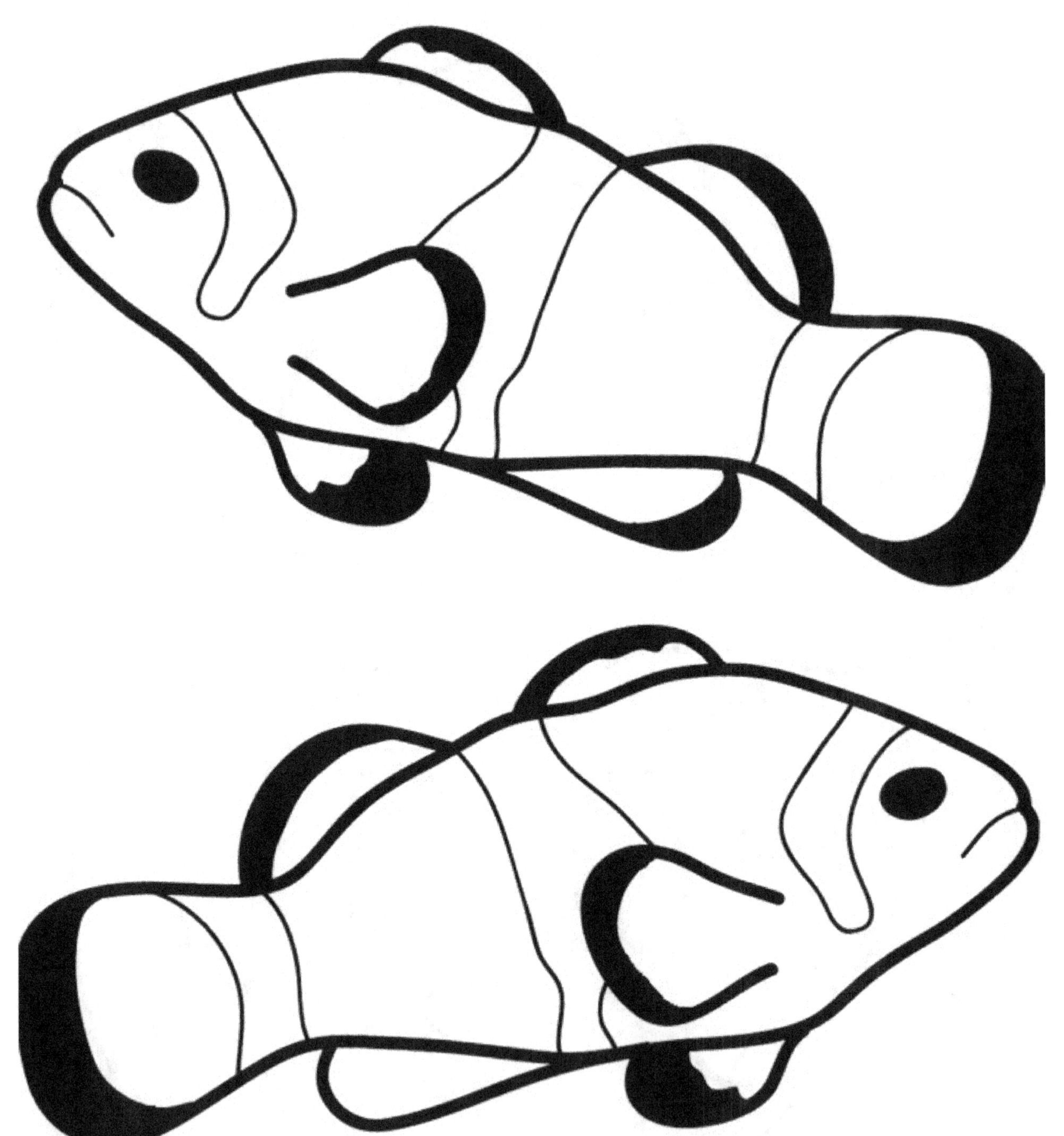

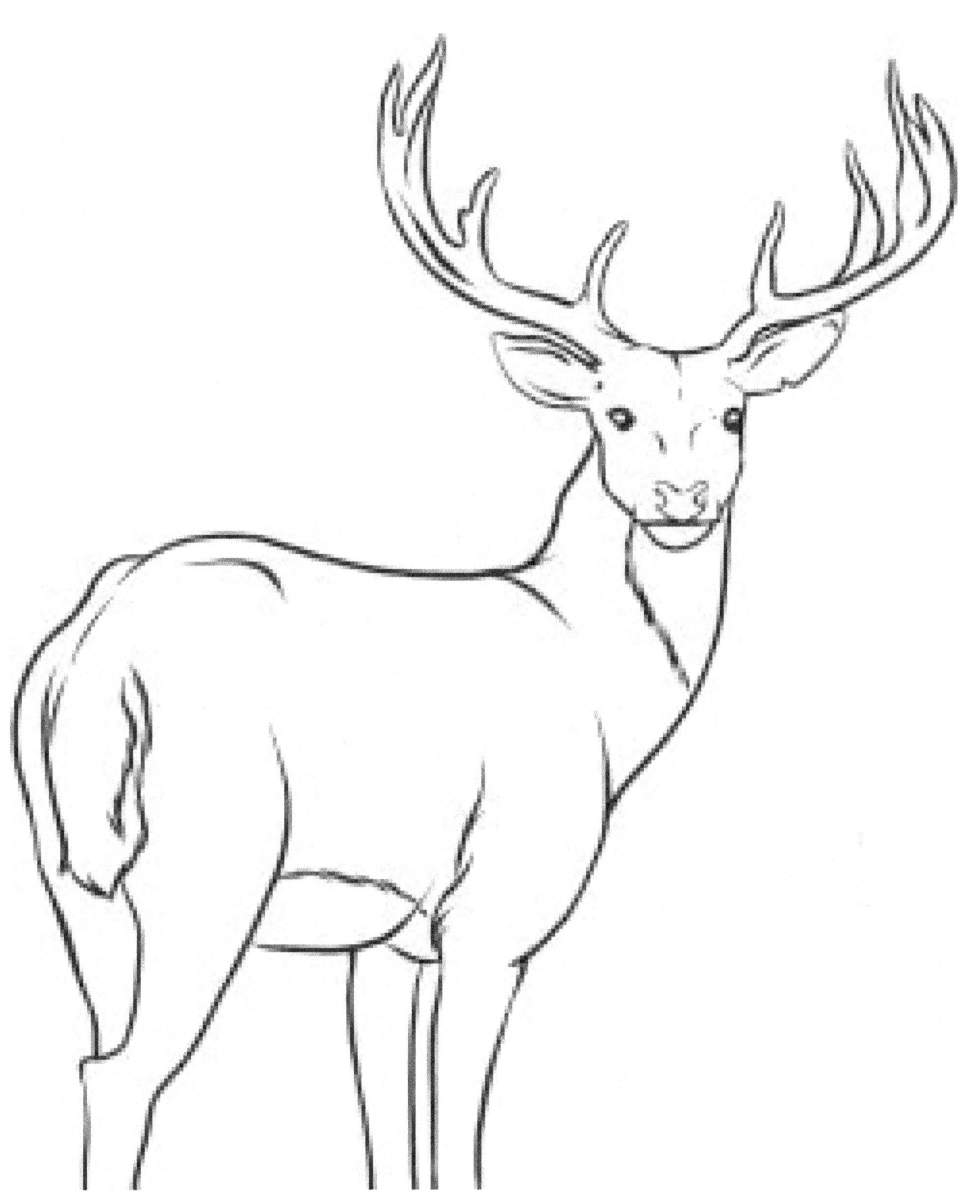

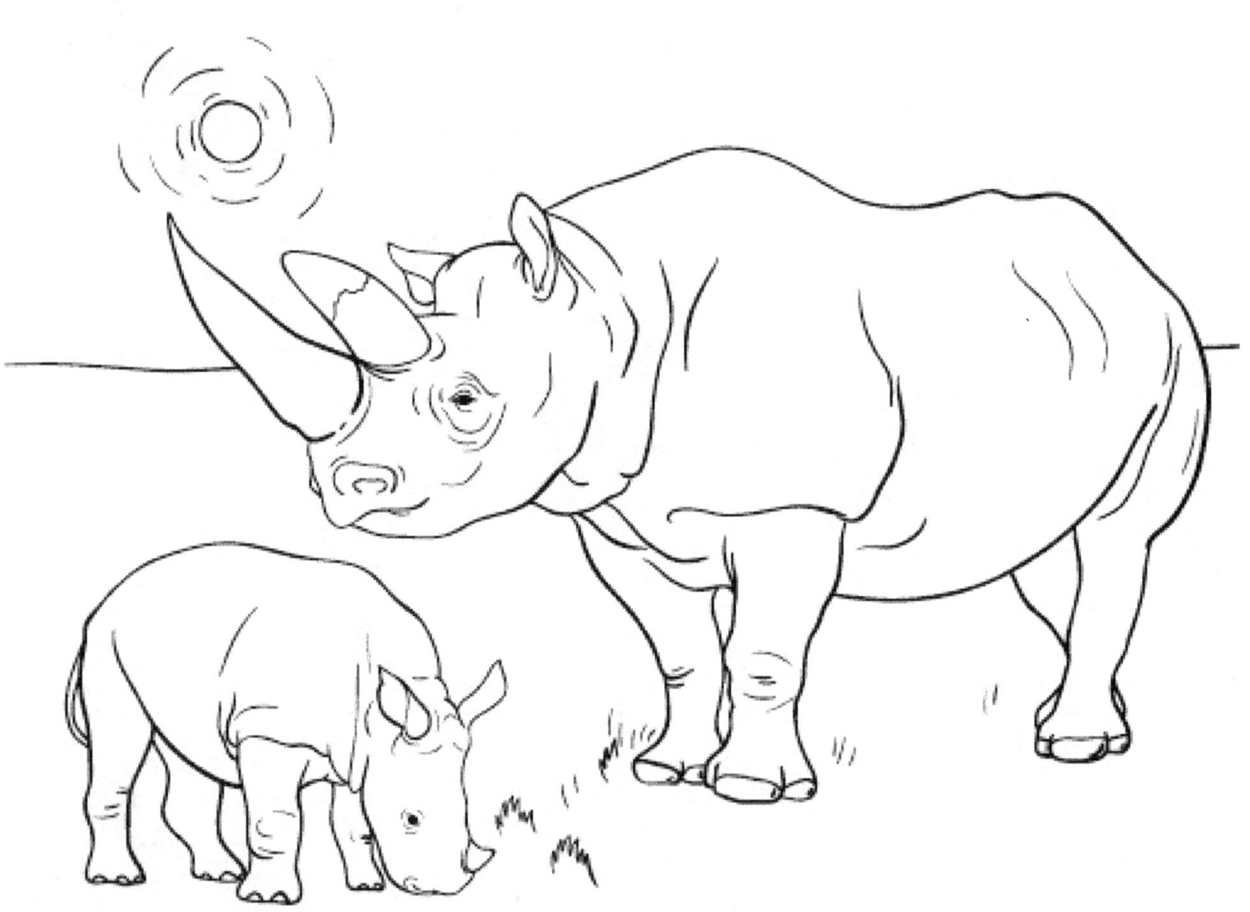

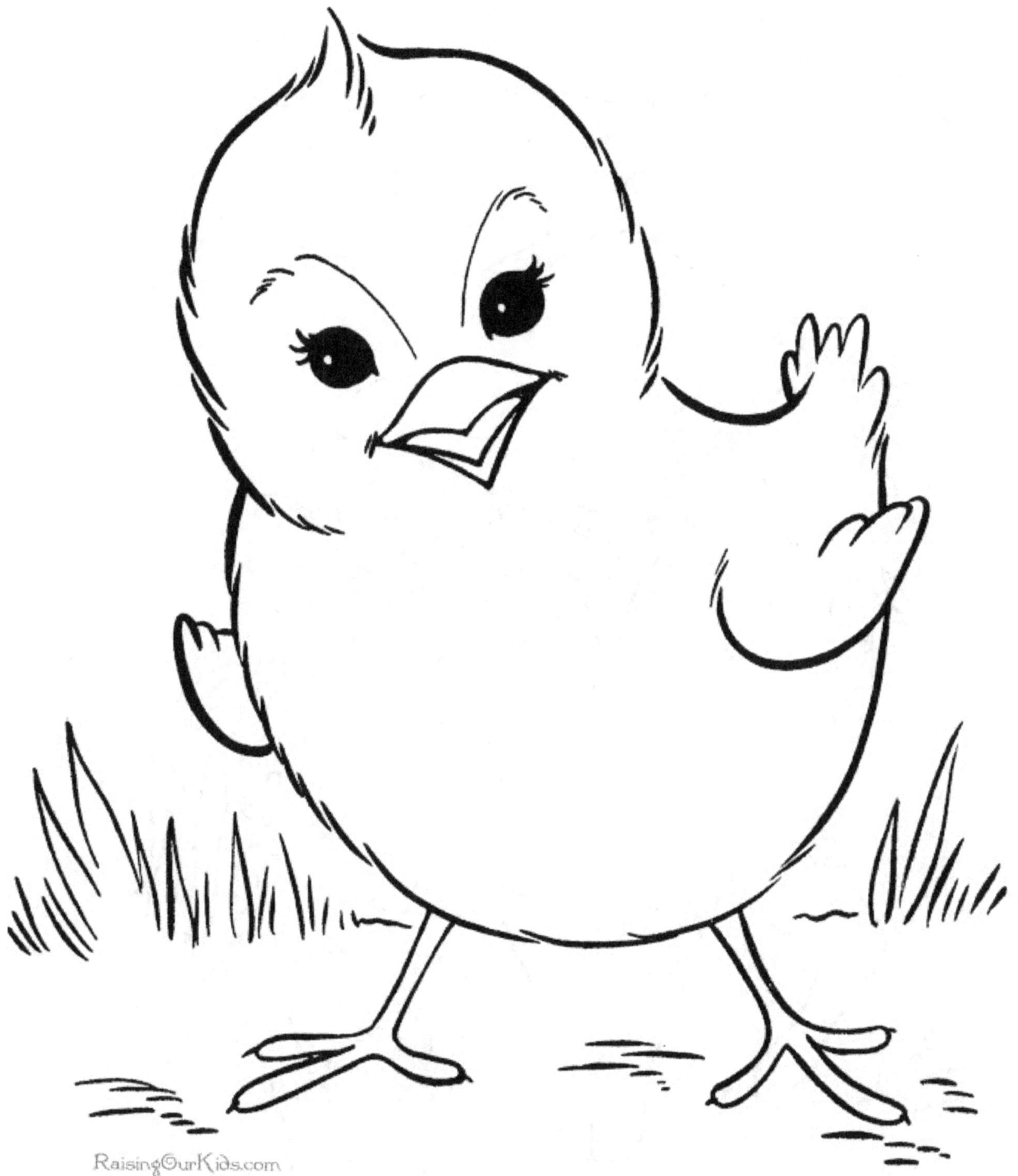
RaisingOurKids.com

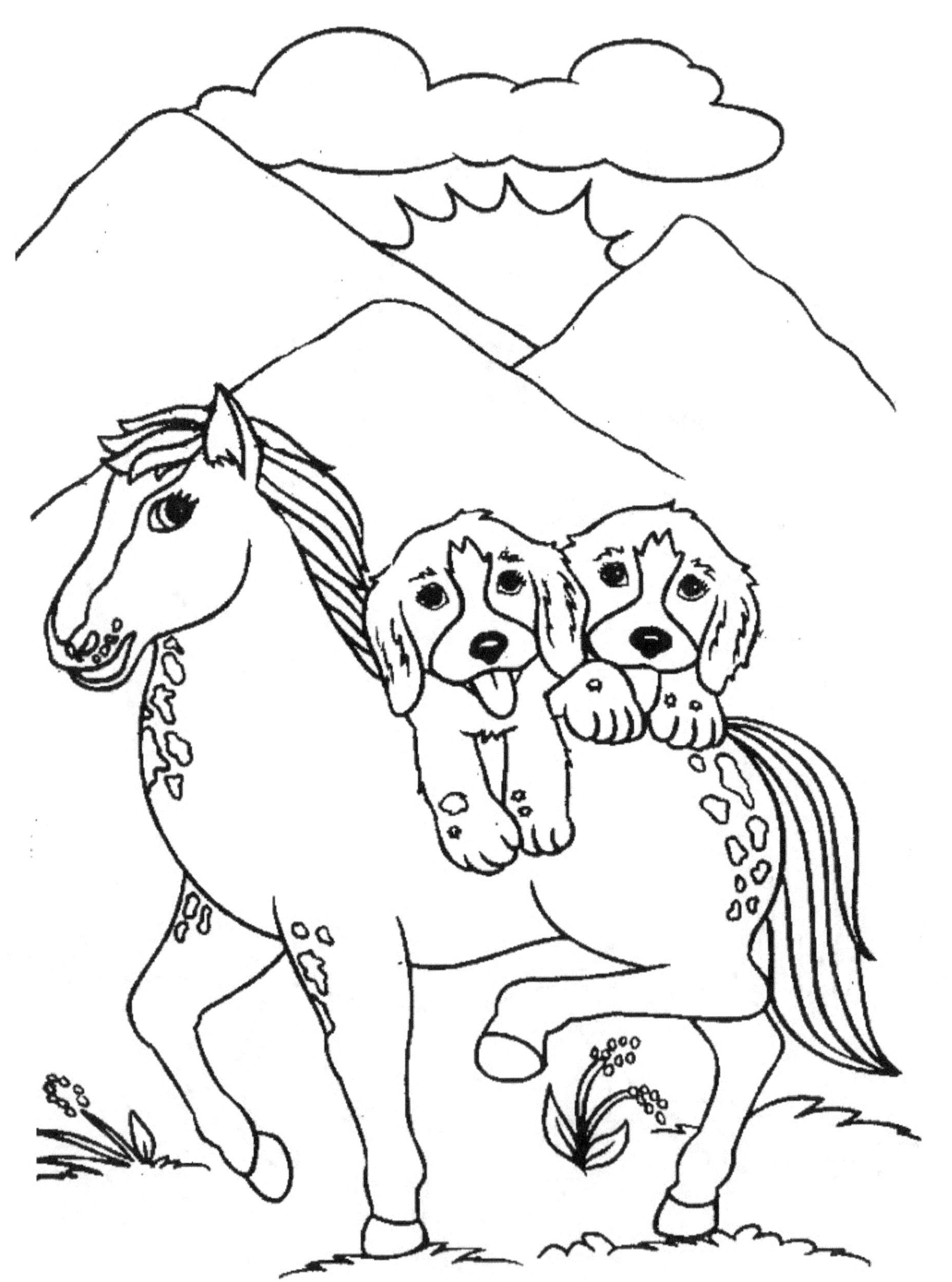

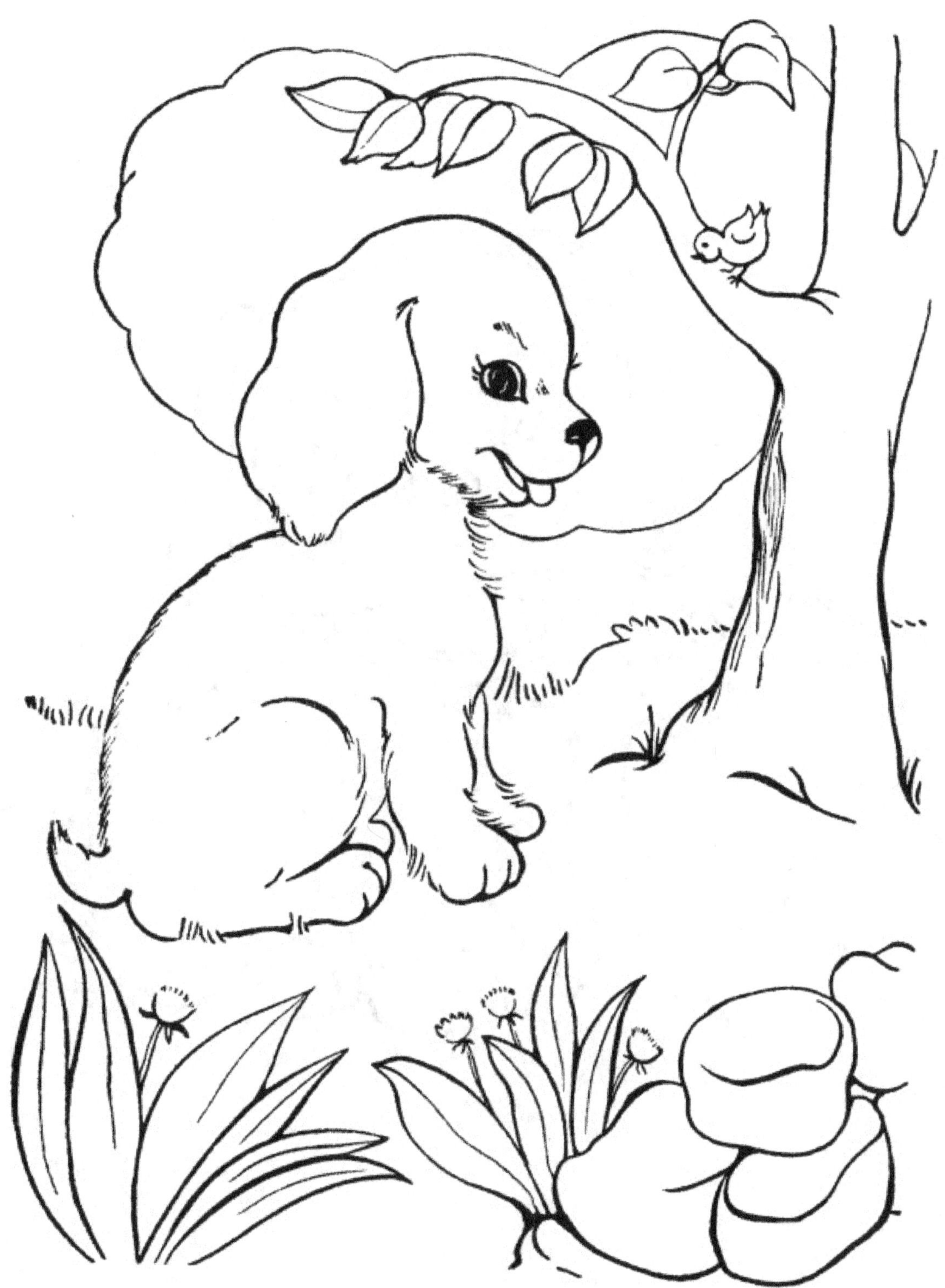

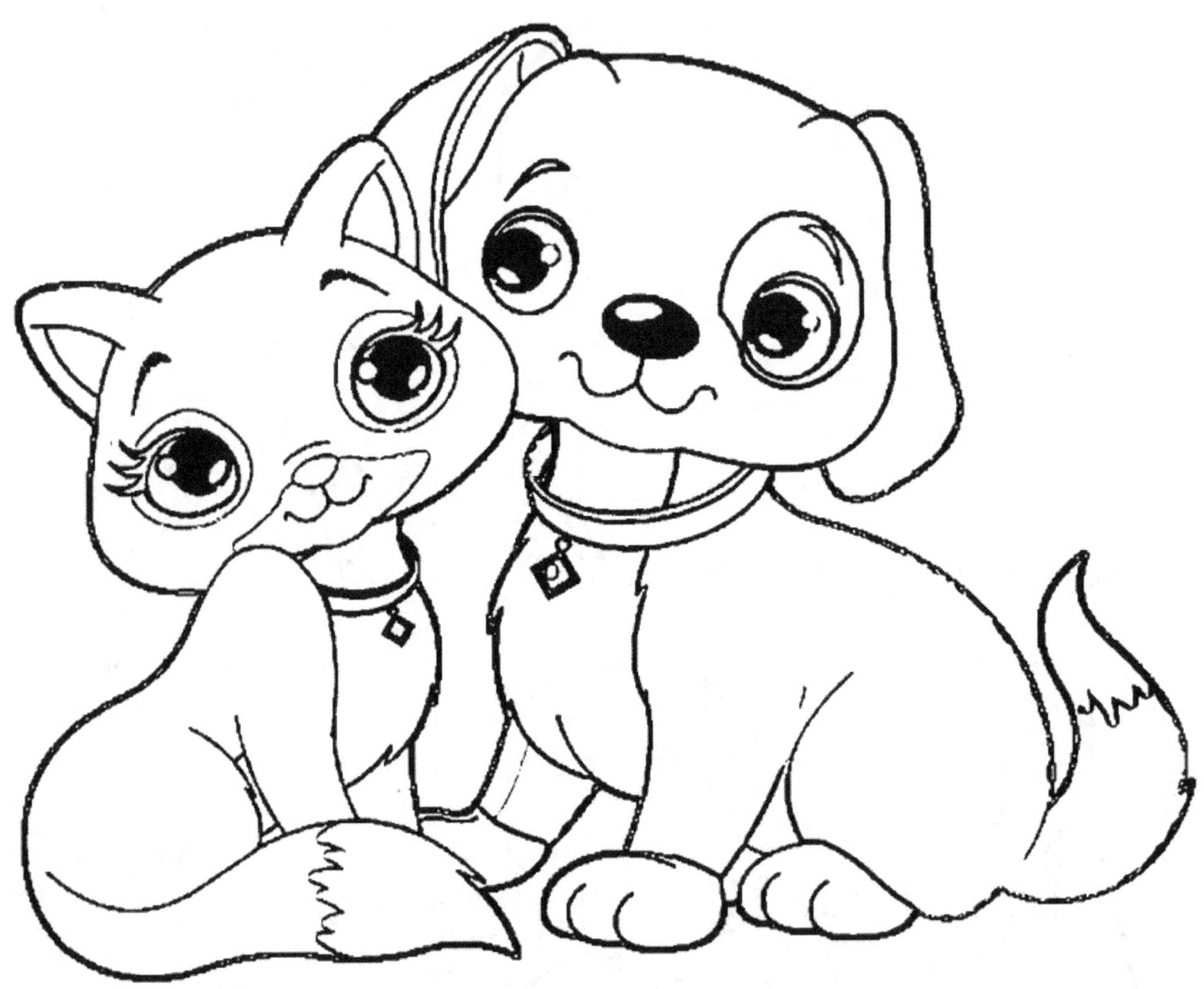

Coloring

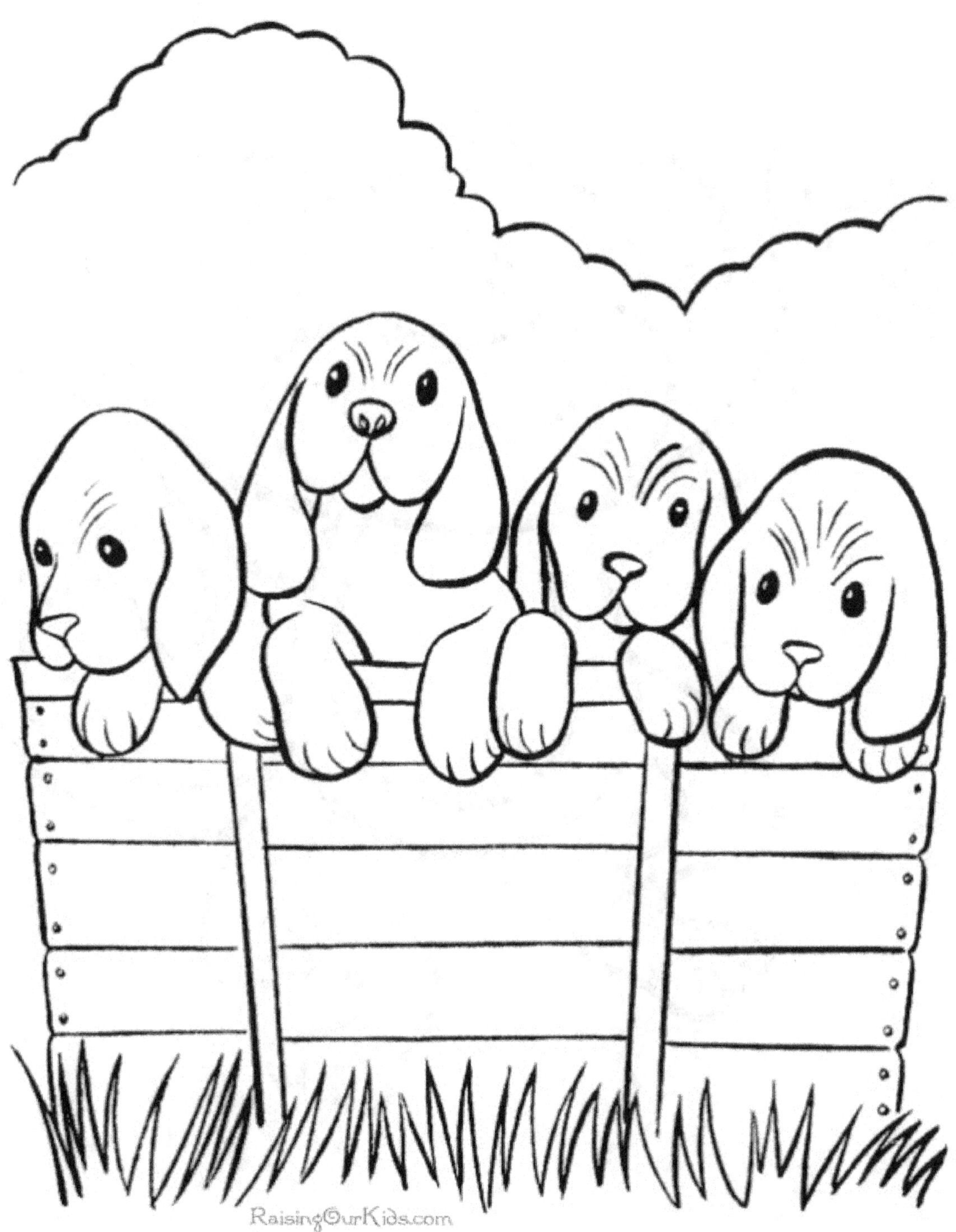
RaisingOurKids.com

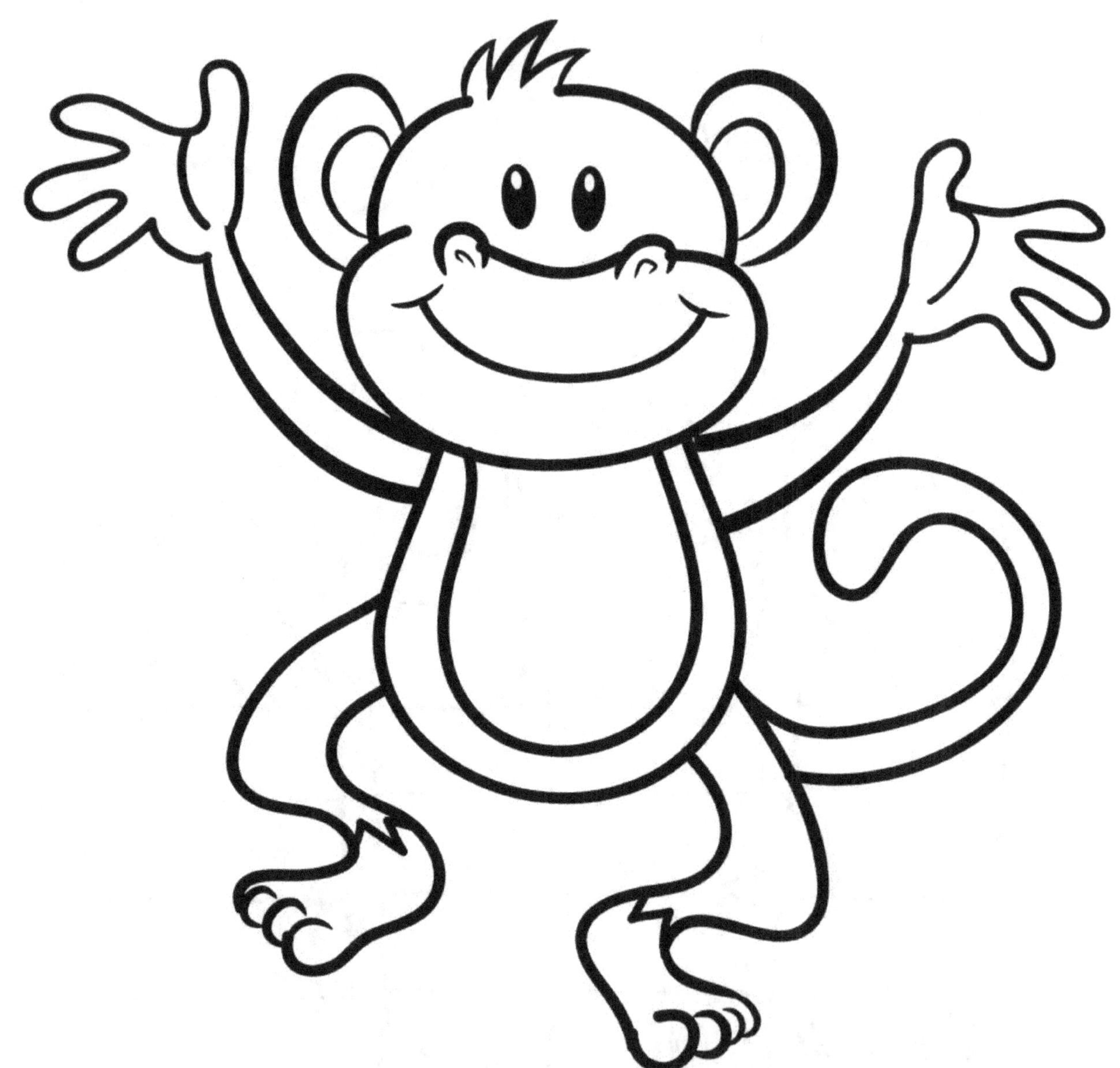

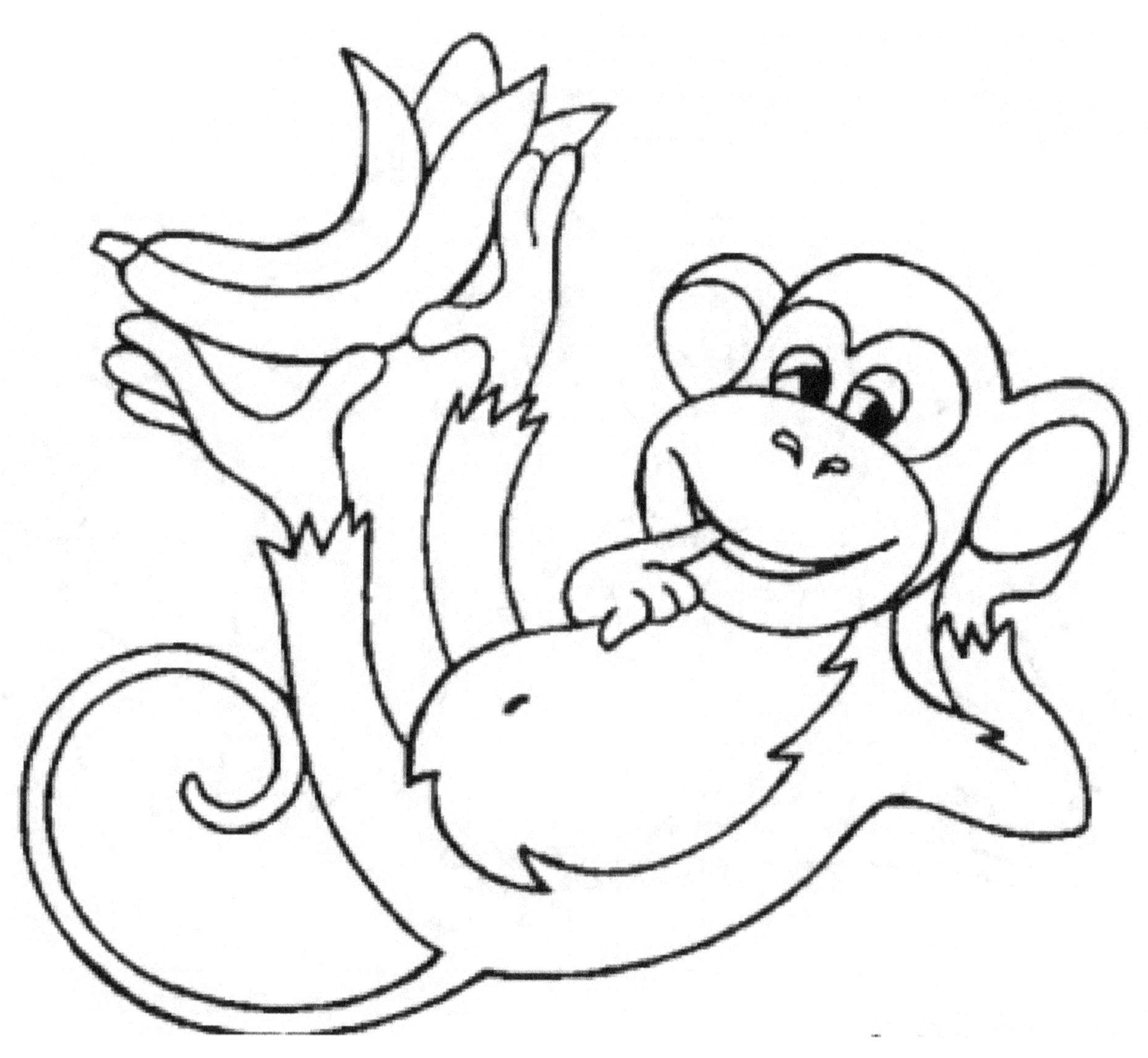

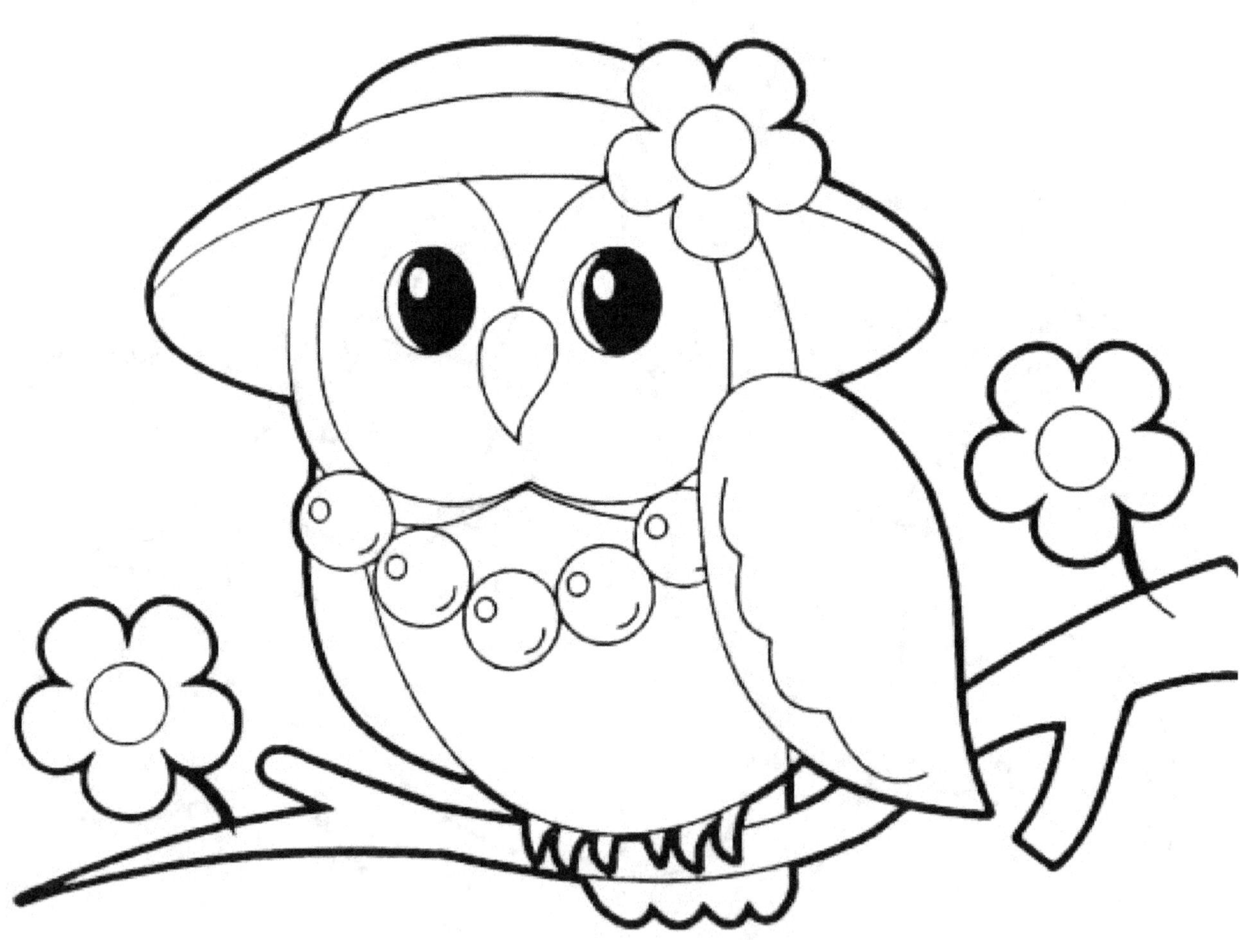

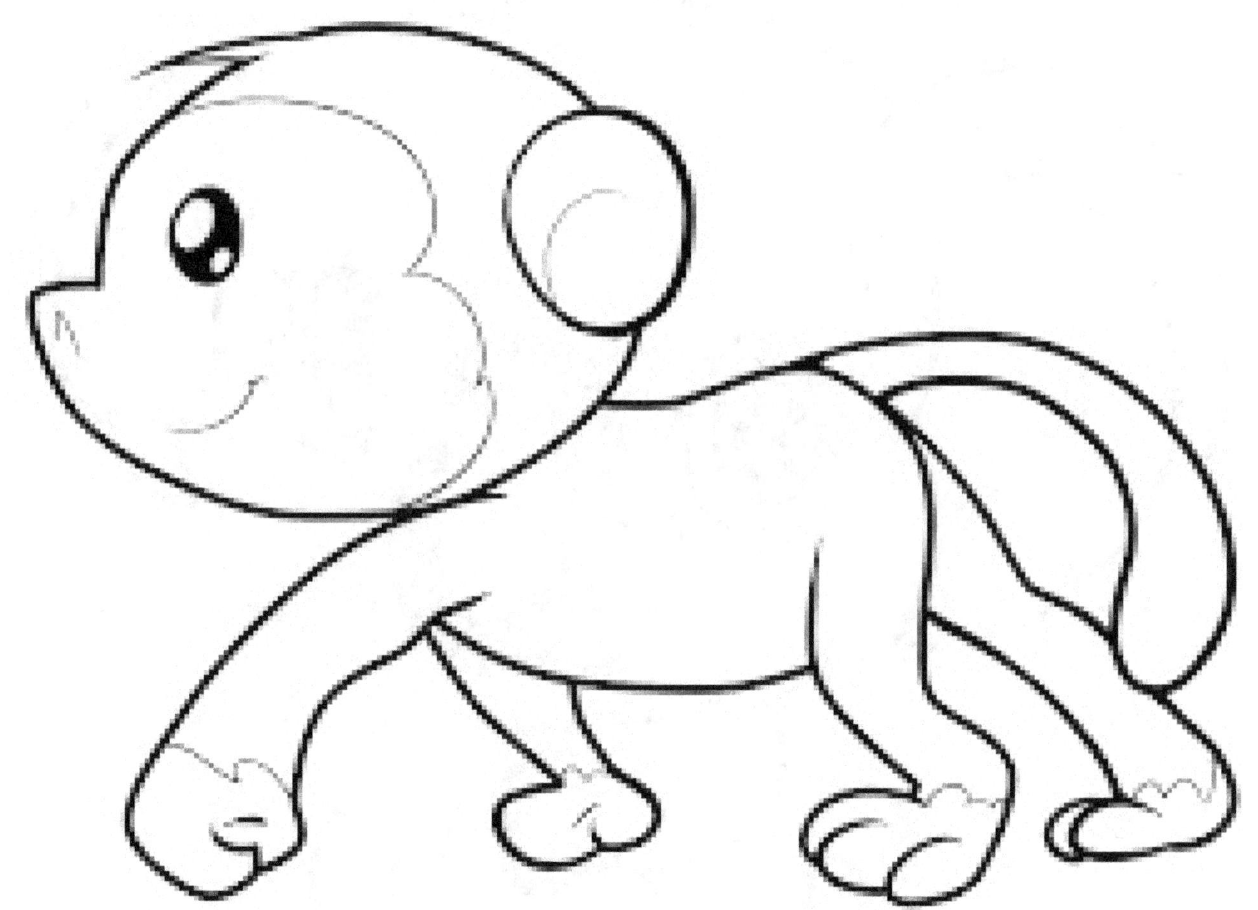

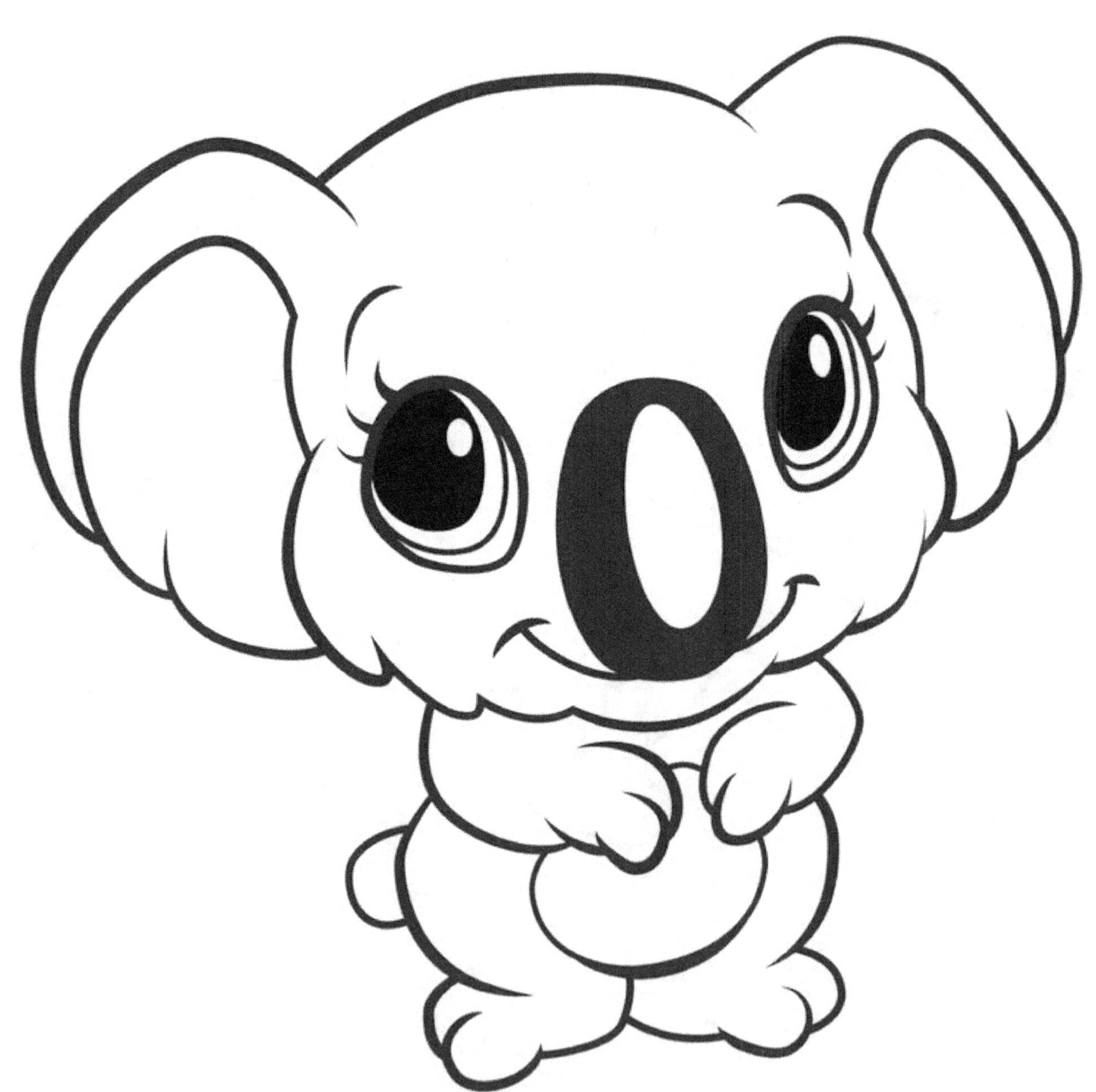

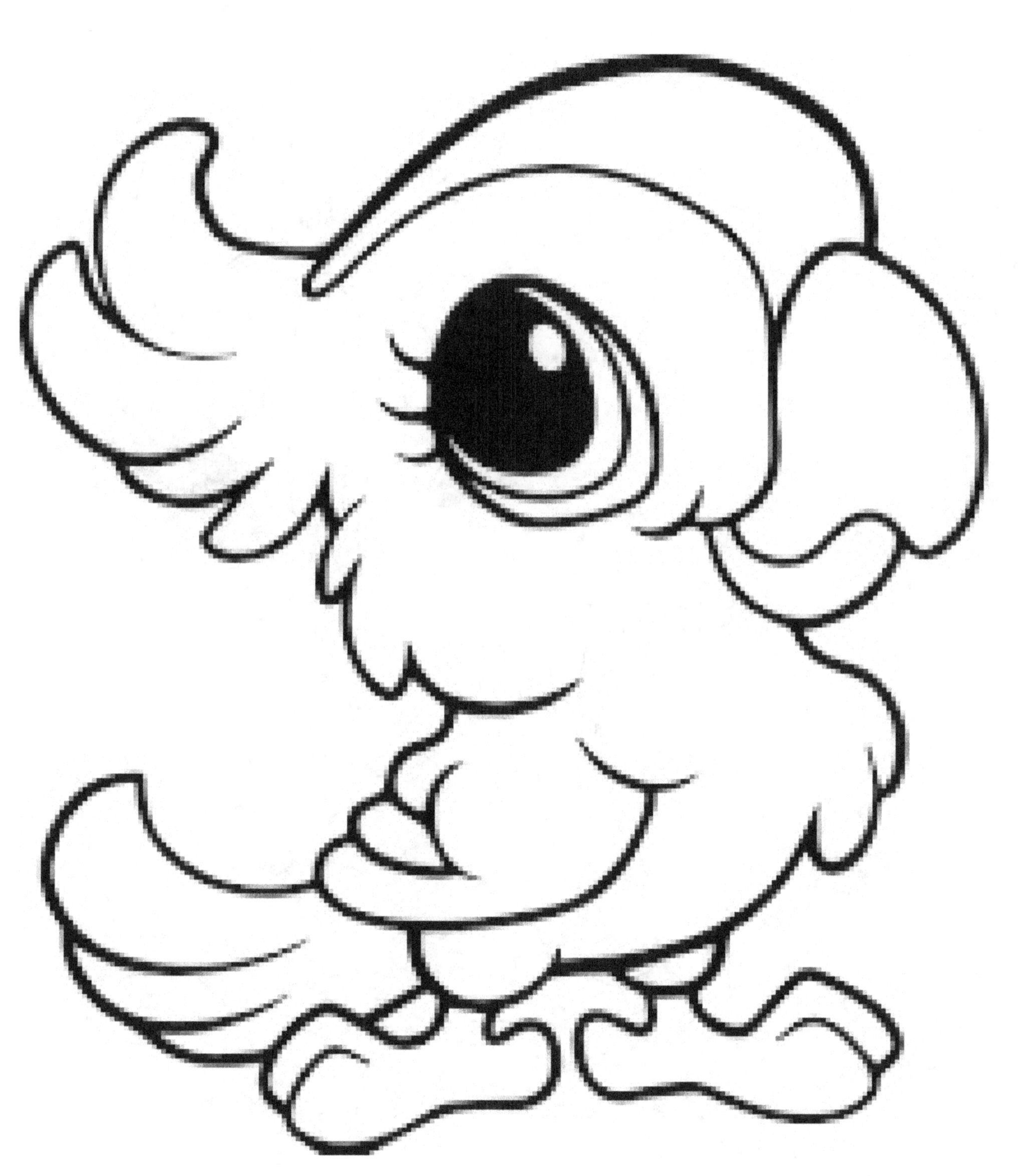

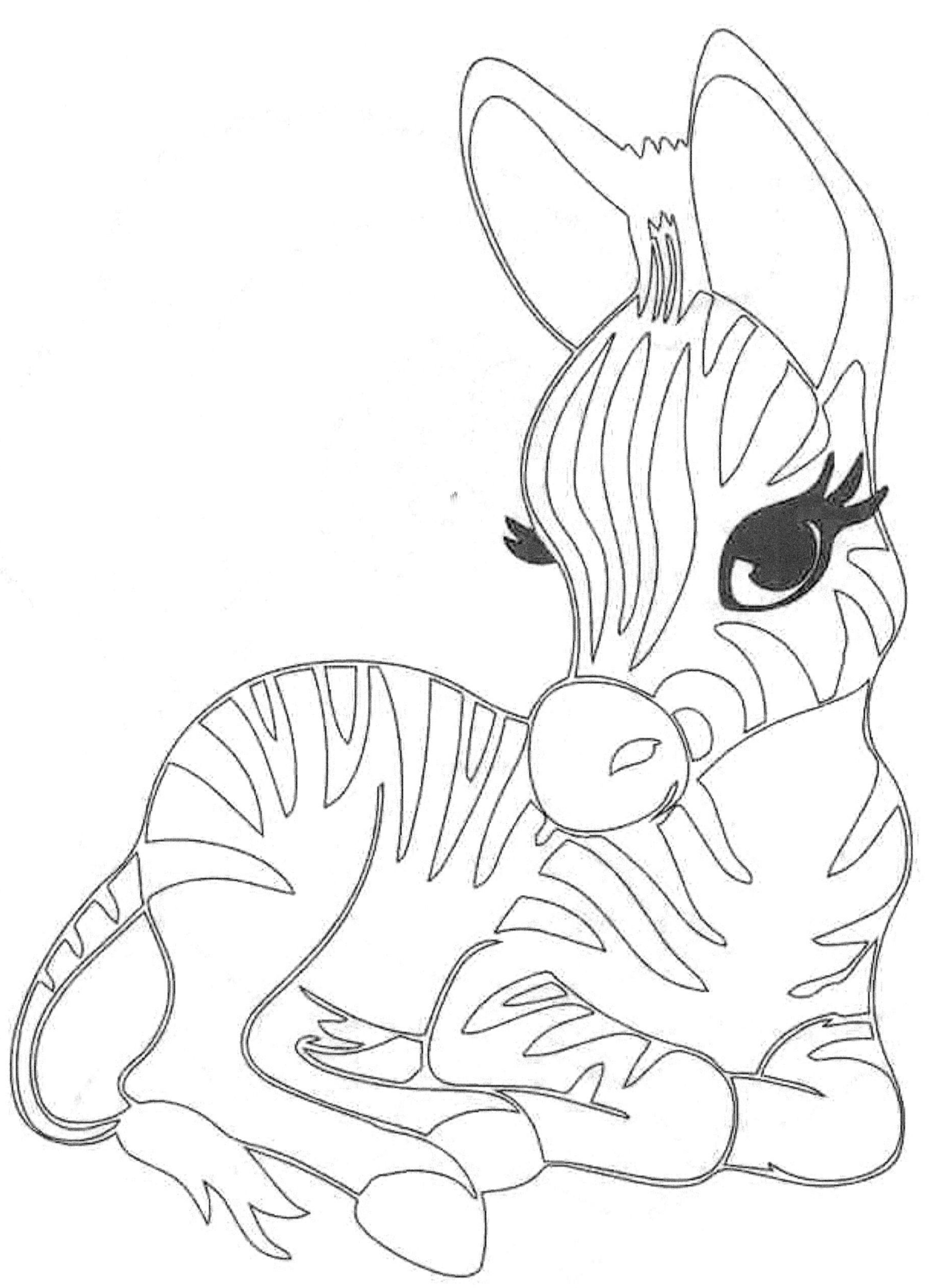

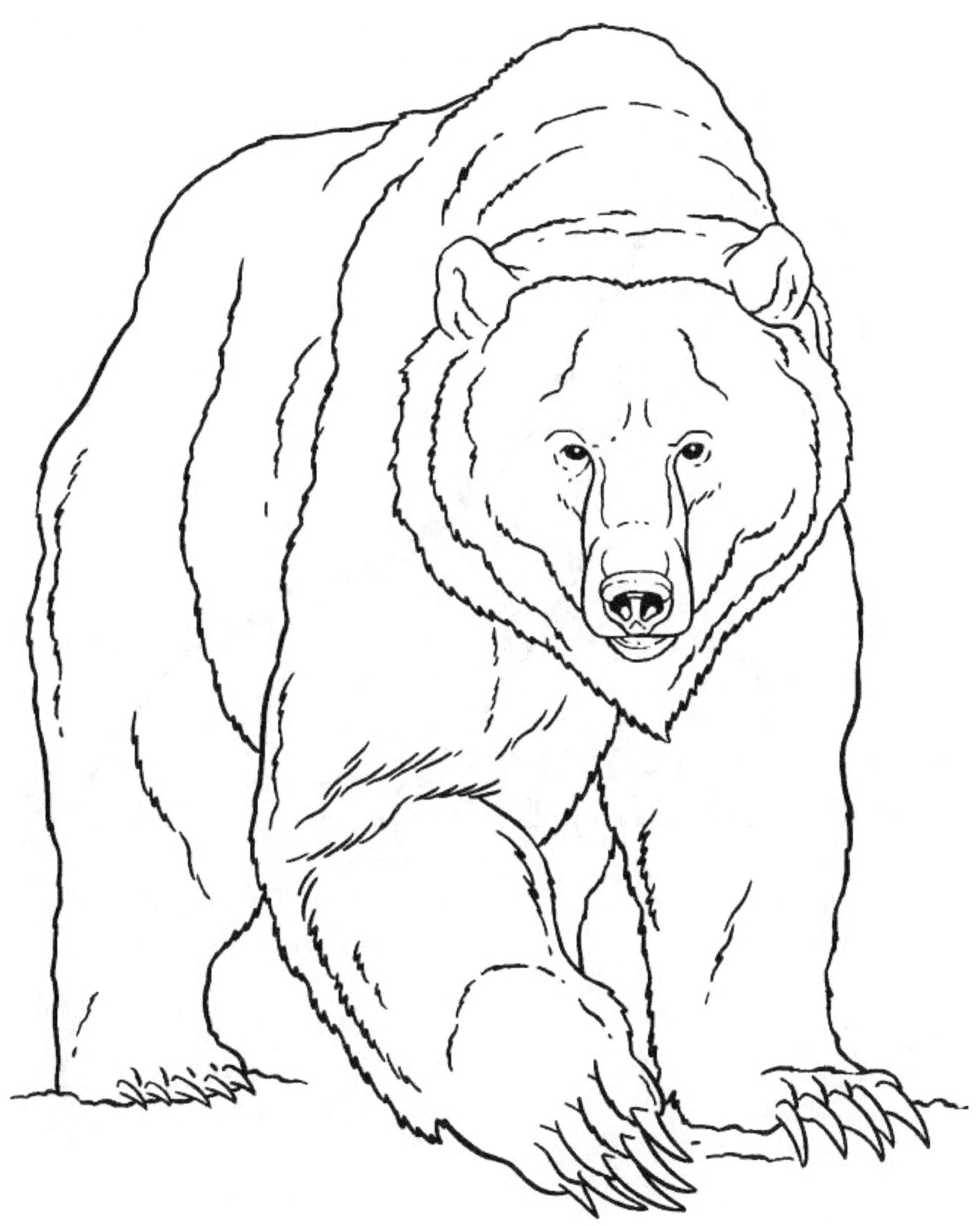

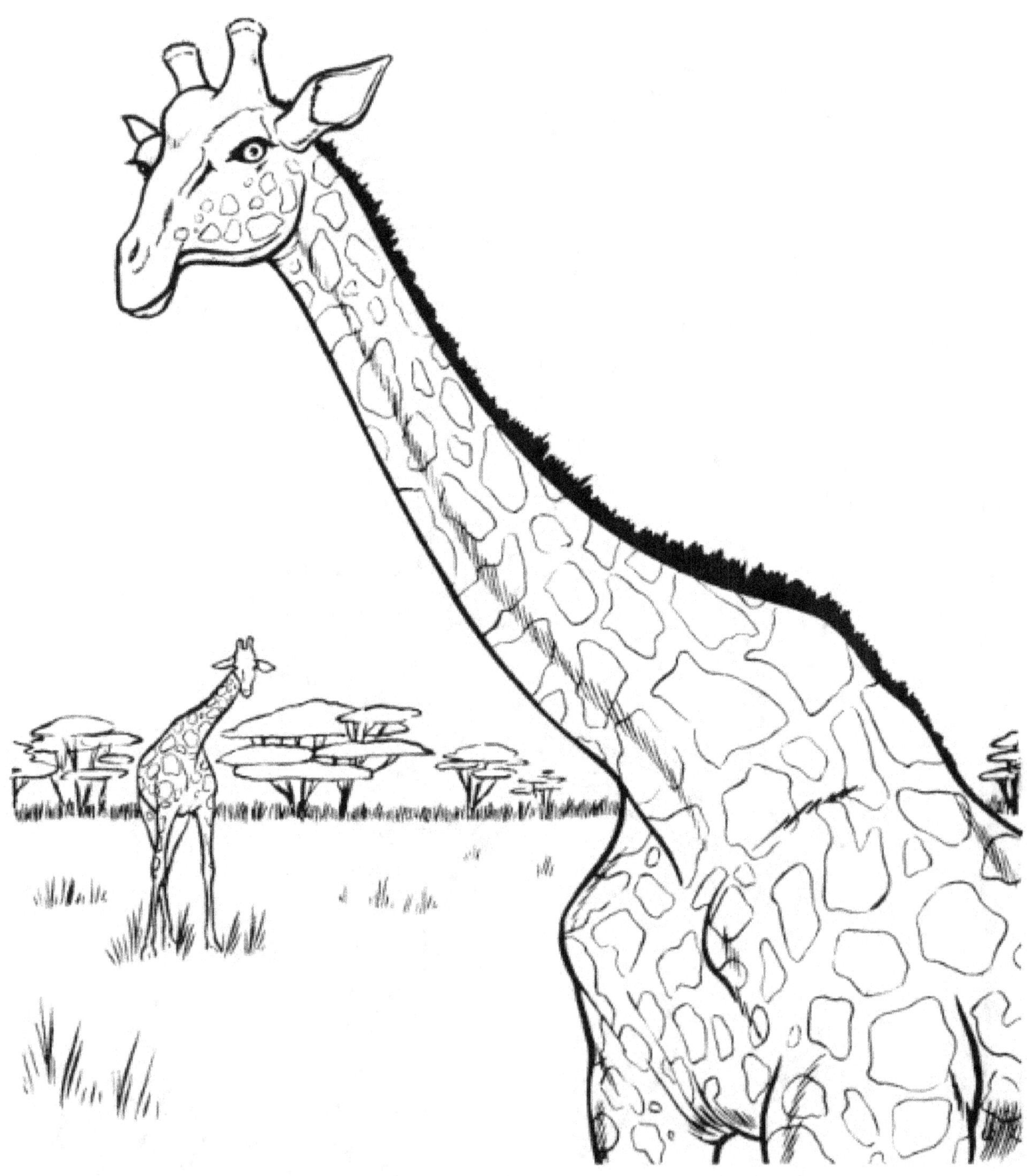

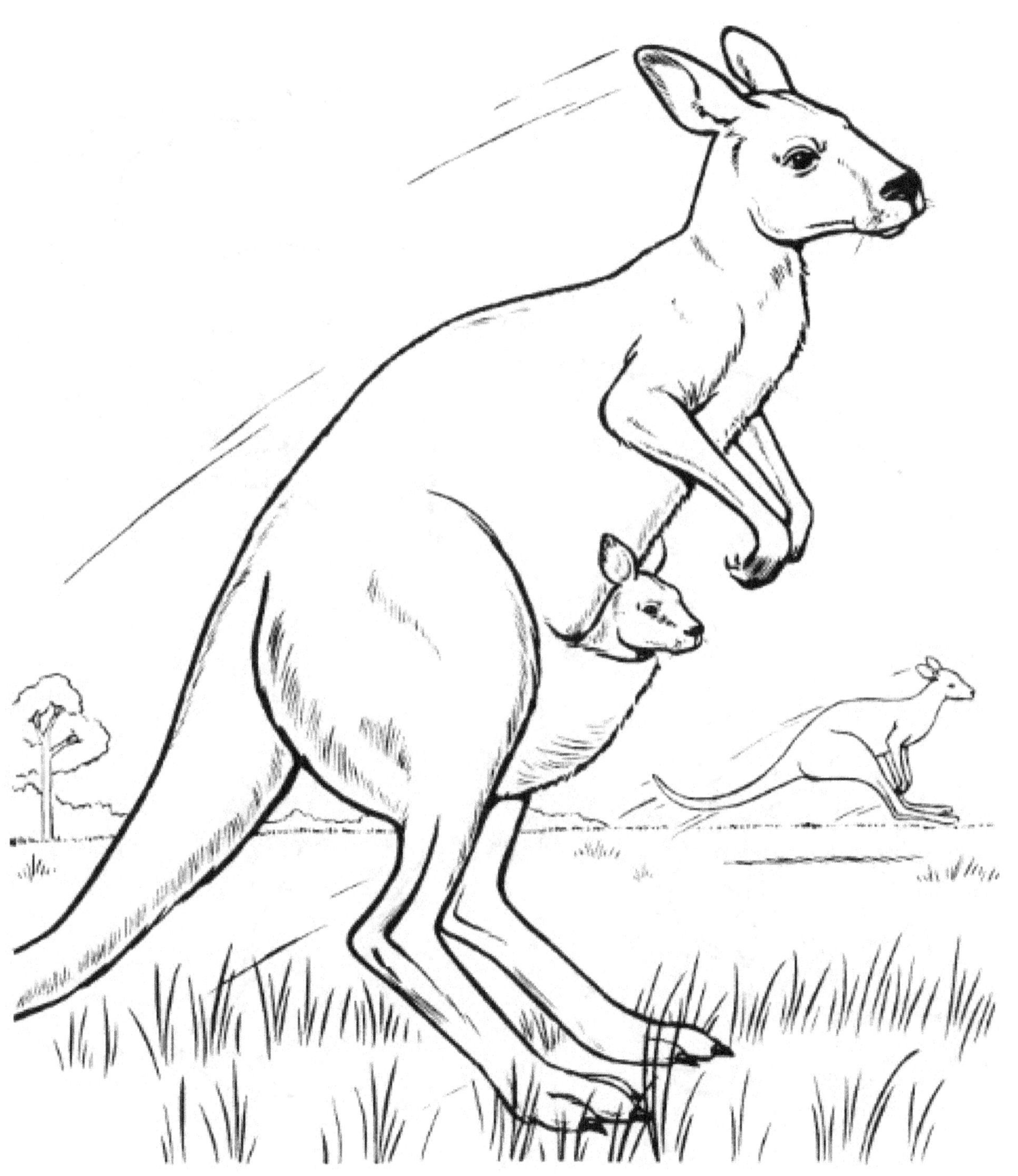

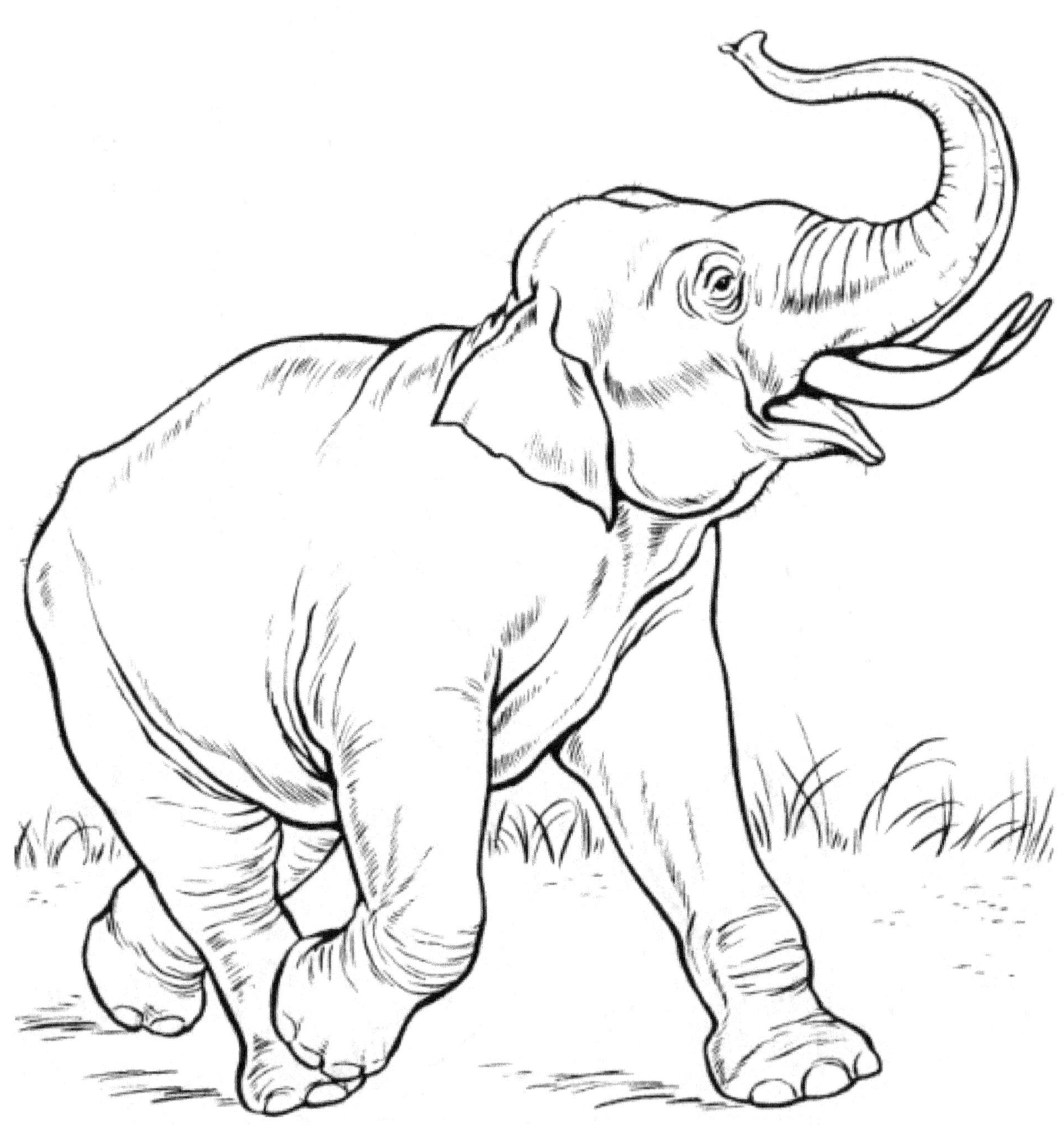

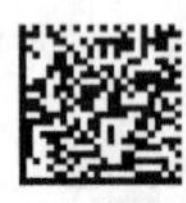